Here's to a

prosperous future!

Ted Jerle

REAL LIFE, REAL MONEY:

100 SMART MONEY MOVES

TO MAKE RIGHT NOW!

Ted Jenkin, CFP®

With Foreword by Fran Tarkenton

Real Life, Real Money:
100 Smart Money Moves To Make Right NOW!

Ted Jenkin

ISBN-13: 978-1517353766
ISBN-10: 1517353769

Table of Contents

Chapter 5: What Uncle Sam Doesn't Want You to Know   106

Chapter 6: Love, Marriage... and Divorce   130

Chapter 7: Managing the Rising Cost of College   152

Chapter 8: 10 Smart Money Moves for Entrepreneurs   176

Foreword by Fran Tarkenton

In the years I've known Ted Jenkin, the biggest thing I've seen is just how much he cares about helping people. And in business—any business—that's what it's all about. We have to help people, and think about others more than ourselves. That's what Ted does, and it has helped him become very successful and, more importantly, help a lot of people improve their lives.

Ted is a real financial guru, and he is incredibly generous with his knowledge and expertise (not to mention his time). Many in the Atlanta area will recognize him from his regular appearances on local radio stations, offering valuable financial advice over the airwaves. I first met Ted after he began writing articles for one of our small business websites. Before long, we were finding opportunities to work together and collaborate anywhere and everywhere. I had him on my radio show. He allowed us to bring in a team of people and film him talking about his business. He came to our offices and filmed another hour-long interview all about personal and business finance. He's been available for webcasts, phone calls, you name it. In these and every other interaction I've had with Ted, he has not only been available, but he's been willing and happy to share something new, something that will give people the information they need to take control of their financial futures. It's always a pleasure to bring Ted in on a new project, because I know that he will have something fresh and insightful—and I'll get to learn just as much as anyone!

One of the things I think you'll notice in this book is that Ted not only has great knowledge, but he's a great communicator. There are so many people who might have great ideas but aren't able to express those ideas in a way that the rest of us can understand and implement. But Ted has the gift of being able take a complex idea and break it down into something that is clear and practical for everyone, not just fellow financial experts. That's what sets this book apart, the easy understanding while still talking about complex ideas.

The world is a very different place from when I was just starting out as a young man in the 1960s, but this is exactly the kind of insight I would have loved to have gotten back then. When I was first drafted out the University of Georgia to play quarterback for the Minnesota Vikings in 1961, I didn't become a millionaire overnight (or even the inflation-adjusted equivalent). In fact, my starting salary was $12,500. I worked every offseason, with multiple jobs. I worked for a trucking company, knocking on doors of shipping clerks. I gave speeches, at $25 a speech. I worked for a printer. I went to work for Coca-Cola. It wasn't just handed to me; even as an NFL quarterback I had to think about and work hard to take care of my personal finances. The advice Ted offers is exactly the kind of thinking people need to reach their goals.

Today we face a new set of challenges. The pension plans of yesterday are disappearing, if not entirely vanishing, changing the way we think about long-term financial planning and retirement. The whole notion of the "gig economy" is changing the way we work, not necessarily working at a job for a company, but taking on projects and doing all different things at different times. And we have a growing group of entrepreneurs trying to juggle both personal and business finances at the same time.

Innovation is the name of the game; nothing stands still for long. With so much happening, it is absolutely essential to take control and have a financial plan in place. Some people might ask if this is the case even for young families. I would say this is important especially for young families. The faster you can get on the right track, the farther along you can go. The longer you are going about blindly, not only is that time you're not spending going the right way, but it also means time lost backtracking from errors and misjudgments.

Ted Jenkin has the right ideas for families looking to get a handle on their personal finances, and he understands today's economy and financial world better than anyone. By following the advice he gives in Real Life, Real Money, you give yourself the best chance to succeed. I think that's an easy choice for anyone.

Introduction

We live in the most educated society in the history of the United States. There are more college graduates, more MBAs, and more PhDs than ever before in the history of our country. Yet, we have more bankruptcies, more credit card debt, more student loans, and less money in our personal savings accounts than ever before. Why is this the case? Part of reason for this phenomenon is that with all of our increased education and knowledge, we are never really taught how to manage family finances in our formal schooling. Personal finance isn't part of the "normal" high school curriculum and for the hundreds of thousands of dollars we spend on college education there isn't even a Personal Finance 101 course offered at most institutions of higher learning. This dearth of education in the marketplace is what spurred me on to write Real Life, Real Money – to give you the tips, techniques, and training so you can make great strides toward improving the bottom line of your personal finances.

My financial industry career began in 1991 after graduating from Boston College. Since then, I've learned a thing or two, getting six advanced designations including the CERTIFIED FINANCIAL PLANNER™ professional certificate (CFP®). The past several years I've been writing a weekly blog for the Wall Street Journal, have become the weekend edition personal finance guru for Headline News on CNN, and my personal finance blog www.yoursmartmon-eymoves.com has soared to the top of the online lists.

Getting good at managing your personal finances it not an easy task by any stretch of the imagination. While the Internet has become a source of information available at our fingertips, it hasn't exactly made many of us better with our own money management. The reason most money books fail is that they don't take into account the challenges we face in real life. Those challenges include considerations like whether to send our kids to private school or public school or whether or not it's a good idea to continue with the private tennis or karate coach. We are faced with issues like how much to spend on a birthday party for an eight year old and how to combat the mental images of friends and family alike who on social media appear to be having a better financial life than you do (even as you try to convince yourself that surely cannot be the case).

When I graduated from Boston College, I went to work for a company called IDS Financial Services, which quickly became the large financial services company American Express Financial Advisors. I didn't have more than a few hundred bucks in my bank account, so my mother was kind enough to make a small down payment on my first automobile, a beautiful shiny maroon Dodge Shadow. I promise you it doesn't get any better than that. I managed to find an apartment in some quasi Section 8 housing in the Southside of Boston which I shared with a friend (and his girlfriend) as my own journey started for achieving my dream of fortune and fame. Pretty much my daily diet consisted of the three P's—Potatoes, Popcorn, and Pasta. It's scary to reflect back thinking about the nights of the week when I would relish the fact that Barrett's restaurant (sad that it's gone now) would offer my best meal, which was some tasty appetizers for free and beer at half price. It's no wonder that I spent so much time working. My apartment had a waterbed, a drafting table, and a beautifully constructed cardboard Bed, Bath, & Beyond night table.

I knew I wanted out of this life of being down to my last few bucks, and I was certain someday that I wanted financial independence. I wanted to be able to CHOOSE what I would be doing for work, and not be subject to working for the man. So I went to work as hard as I knew how for IDS Financial Services and made a whopping $24,000 my first year and $36,000 my second year. I almost quit the business a hundred times, but I guess as my first boss told me I was "smart enough to be dumb enough" to keep coming back day-in and day-out while many around me quit and went on to other careers. My first boss also had an interesting saying, "When you think, you weaken the nation." It took me many years to really understand the meaning of this, and when you see some of the principles I discuss in Real Life, Real Money you'll see why our complicated financial markets will make this statement come true.

As time passed, my income progressively grew in size. Within five years I was making $250,000 annual income, within seven years $500,000 annual income, and then ultimately I cracked the $1,000,000 annual income mark, which is a feat that very few people will do in their lifetime. What did making all this money teach me? It taught me very quickly how flawed the thinking is when it comes to most people and how they manage their money.

Like most people who taste success, I also fell into the trap of making some initial poor decisions with money. These included doing a few private investments with people who "knew what they were doing" or had business ideas that truly seemed bullet-proof. Other missteps: Buying a car that was decidedly more expensive than I really needed. Tracking down a watch that I always saw in the Robb Report that I thought would look good on my wrist. Turns out, I don't even wear a watch to work most days of the week. You get the picture. In essence, I fell into the trap that most successful families do which is spending money as fast they earn it. Luckily, I remembered the "pay yourself first rule." I also believed strongly in paying down debt so

I have been able to amass a really healthy net worth along with a business that I own today.

In Real Life, Real Money, I provide ten different chapters with hard-hitting, easy-to-read, easy-to-implement ways to help you get your family finances on track and on your way to becoming a millionaire. If you are a millionaire already, I'll show you how to keep more of your wealth and you will earn the art of playing defense with your money as opposed to shooting for the stars. No matter what your current financial level or expertise at this juncture in your life, my common sense approach to financial planning can help your family increase your cash flow and your overall net worth. It's time to take control of your money before it takes control of you.

Ready to get started? Read on!

Chapter 1

Making Every Day Financial Decisions

It always makes sense to start with the basics. Since this book is about making smart money moves, in this chapter we will delve into the things that all of us encounter in our daily lives with respect to our money. In this chapter, you will find ideas on simple things like saving money when going to the store to buy jerky, the ways that having a money saving mindset can be applied to your overall financial life, as well as habits that can help get you on the road to a brighter financial future. The 10 short sections that make up this chapter are designed to ask questions, provide tips, and generally, work toward helping you create a financial road map that gets you to where you want to go in life.

Ready to roll? Let's get started!

Five Reasons You Aren't Rich... Yet

At some point in their life, everybody has that dream of having enough money to do whatever they want, whenever they want, irrespective of cost. Well, even if you do think about cost, it's the idea of becoming rich enough to walk in and tell your boss this is your very last day. If you want to get rich, here are five things that may be getting in your way from achieving financial independence, purpose, and freedom.

1. You care what your neighbors think.

There are still many people holding on to their overpriced real estate waiting for it to come back. In the meantime, the mortgage, along with all the fixings you really couldn't afford when you bought that house, is killing your bottom line. It's hard to believe that most people are hanging on to those properties today, along with the country club membership, because of their egos and fear about what their neighbors will think. It's hard to swallow your pride because you know your neighbors might gossip about you at the next party in your development or subdivision. Do the right thing. The quicker you get to a manageable house, the quicker you will see your net worth climb.

2. You can't delay gratification.

Since we live in a day and age where people want it yesterday and typically buy new items on credit, learning how to delay gratification is a big part of becoming rich. There are many temptations between new household purchases, fancy vacations, and the latest electronic gadgets. If you limit yourself to just one special item versus many you begin to see the savings instantly. You can have a great vacation or a wonderful household purchase without breaking the bank. For your next temping purchase, just try to wait six more months before you buy it and then ask yourself if you really need it.

3. You don't use the rule of thirds.

One important wealth building strategy I have recommended to clients for years is the rule of thirds. For any bonus, pay raise, etc., you get through work save one-third of that number. You can still have fun with a third of it and a third will likely go to taxes. This strategy will also make sure you don't outstrip your income by expanding your lifestyle too fast.

4. You don't pay attention to your money.

People who tell us that they don't look at their 401(k) statements are destined to not be wealthy. You must act like the CEO of your family/self and pay attention to the fine details if you want to grow your net worth. It won't happen solely by putting it the hands of others. I recommend getting a competent Private CFO® or financial advisor to help, but you must be the owner of your finances.

5. You have bad habits.

At the end of the day, habits are important no matter what you do in life. If you have made money mistakes in the past, then you may feel like it just isn't your thing to be good at money. Changing your attitude can change your altitude when it comes to building your wealth. It takes just 21 days to create a financial habit – and the benefits can be enormous.

Beef Jerky, CVS, and a Pop Math Quiz

Since we are peppered with advertisements today for coupons, deals, and "once in a lifetime" offers, we all have to become smarter consumers and shoppers to make the best financial decisions in our lives. However, since the amount of time we have to get basic tasks done seems to be shrinking every day, we can get trapped in convenience stores by the way they position and market products to us.

My family and I have developed a small addiction to beef jerky, turkey jerky, and any spicy flavor that they come up with these days. If you enjoy eating jerky, you may have noticed the recent spike in prices at grocery and convenience stores alike. One day we had a hankering for some jerky on the way home, so we stopped at a local store to see which package of tasty treats we were going to pick up. Typically, most drugstores and convenience stores will put the "snacks" in one particular area of the store. When we arrived at the section with the beef jerky, we noticed that the prices were as high as anytime we could remember. One package of regular Jack's Links Beef Jerky was $6.49 for 3.25 oz. Now, CVS does sell packages with more than 3.25 oz., but there isn't much of a material savings for buying the larger packages. We wondered if it was really a smart money move to spend $6.49 just to satisfy our craving for a little beef jerky.

I decided to meander my way over to the new area at CVS called "$10 for 10 items". You might notice that at major grocery stores and drugstores like CVS, they will create these areas to offload proprietary products or offer some type of deal on one of your favorite treats. After perusing this section, seeing all types of snacks, we noticed a small section with some individually wrapped Jack's Links Beef Jerky. The same regular flavored Jack's Links Beef Jerky could be purchased at $1 for .8oz of beef jerky. If you do some simple math, that means we could buy 3.2oz of beef jerky for $4 instead of paying $6.49 for the same product three aisles over in CVS. Why in the world would the same company offer the same product in two different places at different prices?

Grocery stores are famous for this, but other types of convenience stores are catching on to the way we shop as customers. They know with your busy lives that you often will not even go in every aisle in the store. In fact, you'll likely know what you were coming to the store for when you pulled into the parking lot. Thus, they assume that you think they have already given you the best price possible or you will get it at the counter with their store discount card. Wrong!!! Companies will trick you into this all the time. Do yourself a favor and anytime you go shopping start your process in the "deal aisle" – that could be the "$10 for 10 items" or "dollar days" or whatever the company calls its deal section. There may not be a deal on any products you like or you can find out just like we did that you can save 40% just by walking from one part of the store to the other.

Three Money Lessons I Learned From My Parents

Often we don't appreciate everything that happens to us growing up. We know that our formative years can very much outline and shape the way we think and act as an adult. We know that in some households money never gets discussed with the kids, and in others there are detailed discussions about how to create a household budget. These money lessons we learn as kids have a much deeper meaning in how we think about money than we can ever know in our adult years. Here are three money lessons learned as a kid and how they shaped our thinking around handling family finances today.

LESSON #1: Credit Card Debt

Unfortunately, credit card debt is a learned habit in many families, For example, a parent might enjoy buying things before they actually earned them. They may spend a great deal of money on credit cards for vacations, sporting event tickets, or hobbies. Often times, a parent may hide their excessive credit card use from the rest of the family and far too often, families learn about the debt after the parent passes away. This lesson is a tough one to learn, so if you grew up in a family with credit card debt, learn the lesson and not the habit.

LESSON #2: No New Cars

Imagine this: Every three to four years, your mother and father go out and purchase a brand new car. The father loves getting a new car. As a kid, you don't really think about things like depreciation and how a new car is one of the worst financial assets to spend money on unless you want to guarantee yourself that you'll lose money. No matter how good the car may make you feel, it cannot add to your bottom line. Now, with my own family finances we will only purchase automobiles that are two to three years old. Although we could easily afford to buy a new car for cash, we know the better financial decision is to let the basic wear and tear take place before we purchase the car.

LESSON #3: Allowances
This is really interesting because kids used to actually get an allowance in their household for doing the handful of chores that were assigned to them. It began as a few bucks per week and got up to $10 a week when they were in high school. However, there were weeks where the kids really didn't do all the chores and the parents would still give the kids money if they needed it, despite the fact that the chores were not completed. As a family today, my wife and I decided that for our kids there would be no allowance. Chores are expected responsibilities with all family members and you don't get paid to do what is expected of you. People have varying views on this, of course. Some don't pay for chores or grades, because as kids they learned that this might not be the best incentive award.

What money lessons did you learn from your parents growing up as a kid?
Did you get an allowance?
Did your parents pay for all of your college education or pay nothing at all?
Were there money arguments between your parents?
Did you get many gifts during your birthday or very few gifts?
How were parties handled in your household?
Did you pay for your first car?
What was a typically dining out experience?

All of these questions and more have shaped the way you will handle your money and potentially how you go about doing what you do for your kids. It's amazing that money lessons often create a reverse psychology in you as a grown adult. It's the age-old "I don't want to do what my parents did to me" attitude that we can carry within us whether it comes to spending money on vacations, eating out, or our children. Just remember that kids pick up everything and the way you talk about money in your household will have a big impact in the way your kids handle their money in the future. The lessons learned both good and bad have greatly shaped our attitude toward money decisions today. Think about the money lessons you learned in your household growing up and decide how you incorporate those values in your life today.

Five Disastrous Financial Moves

If you avoid these five disastrous financial moves, you should have a good chance of becoming prosperous and hitting your goals. If you have made one of these already, it may be time to evaluate how you can get back on track – which may include seeing a financial professional.

1. Buying more home than you can afford.

Buying more home than you can afford will truly cripple your long-term financial plan. Years ago, we heard a very simple financial ratio called the "primary obligation ratio" which said that your mortgage payment shouldn't be much more than 28% to 34% of your total gross monthly income. Use that statistic in conjunction with putting 20% down on your home purchase and you will typically avoid this #1 financial disaster. It is impossible to squeeze into a home financially like you would a car or some other one-time purchase. Many people forget the cost of furnishing the house, which can run 5% to 15% of the home value depending on your taste. While most people think that they can "fill" their home over the rest of their lives, the truth is people work hard to fill their unfinished homes immediately, thus compounding their initially bad decision. In addition, you should estimate that basic upkeep of your home will be between 2% and 4% annually. This goes from landscaping, to basic home repairs, or just re-painting rooms. Many people do not put these costs into their budget when they figure their mortgage payment. Last, for the newly married couple that has two incomes, you should consider what will happen when you have your first child. In many cases, one spouse decides to stay home after the birth of a first child. Beyond the new kid expenditures, the budget could take a huge hit with one less income.

2. Private equity investments with friends.
Sure you will hear the story of some guy who invested in a start-up technology company, a newly developed building, or some fancy new gadget, who made a boatload of money. However, for the regular guys and gals who put money into a friend's start-up restaurant, a piece of land they never saw, or a few shares in a new company, it generally doesn't work out in the long run. The odds of cashing in on a private equity investment are very slim. There is a less than 5% chance that your money will actually come out the back end of the investment; more often the result is a loss of all of the money. Here is our simple rule: If you aren't going to be actively involved in the business as an owner stay away. Unless of course you want to lose your money or have it take 10 years longer than you thought to try and get it back.

3.Carrying credit card debt.
Besides a reasonable home mortgage, most debt just isn't good for you. The one killer is carrying ongoing credit card debt on a long-term basis. Sometimes credit card debt occurs because of some one-time emergency or catastrophe, but more often than not it is just

simply created by living beyond your financial means. You spend more money than you make and do it for a sustained period of time and you end up owing the wrong people. Getting tracked down by a loan shark with the Sopranos won't end up feeling good, and neither does watching your debt compound at an 18% to 24% interest rate with the credit card company. At an 18% interest rate, your debt will double almost every 4 years. The sooner you get a budget and a financial plan, the sooner you will pay off the debt.

4. New automobiles.
Make whatever argument you like; buying a new car is just about the worst investment you can make. We don't mean trading in an older car for a newer "used" car, but just buying a new car period. Think of it this way, if you knew that an investment would go down in value 40% over the first two years, you just simply wouldn't do it. With body styles changing less frequently in cars today, you can settle for getting a car with almost all the new technology and style for 40% less in price. This financial move over 20 years can save you huge money, which you can apply toward your financial goals. Just add a "new car" air freshener if it helps stop buying new automobiles.

5. Not saving enough.
It's true that the markets and economy have been shaky, and could be for many years to come. When you look at a goal like retirement, most of us do not want to retire later nor do we want to live on less after working for 30 or 40 years. Since you cannot control the markets or your overall rate-of-return, the one thing you can do to tip the odds in your favor is save more. Use our simple tip of saving 33% of every raise you get and you will learn to live within your means vs. spending your raises and bonuses. Over time, the money will be out of mind and out of sight, putting you in a position come retirement time.

Money Unhappiness? It's All About Expectations

Every year that the birthday clock turns over, it is smart to ask ourselves one simple question: "Are we getting any wiser?" Many say that gaining wisdom in life is far more powerful than any bit of knowledge that you can acquire. Of course, you can know a lot of information about many different subjects, but the key to making progress is about applying your wisdom to situations for the best possible outcome. I've come to the conclusion around one very key piece of information with an extremely simple statement: Happiness or unhappiness is all about expectations, met or unmet. This statement can be instrumental in handling financial fights and crises in your household because, if you dig deep, you'll find that your current state of mind is all about how you feel – it's about the bar of expectations that were set for you or those that you set yourself. Let's take a look at how to apply this piece of wise advice so you can become happier in your life.

1. The spender/saver couple.

When a married couple splits, there are many factors that can cause the break up. However, personal financial matters are among the leading reasons that create Splitsville. This is why when you get married, or if you are currently married, discussing your financial goals is extremely important. It's also imperative that you figure out how you are going to handle money matters, and what types of purchases truly matter to you as a family. For example, you may expect to send your children to the college of their choice while your spouse is thinking just to give the kids a head start of $10,000 when college begins. Without setting agreed expectations through an overt conversation, consider the battle that will ensue down the road. What if you believe that wearing brand-named clothes will increase your children's popularity in school and your spouse does not? With words unspoken about this type of subject, ill will can be harbored for many years before a verbal explosion happens between the two of you. The key is that even if you don't 100% agree in principal, it is crucial to set expectations about where the spending levels should occur so your blood pressure doesn't rise to epic proportions every time you open the credit card bill.

2. The dream home.

Your home will likely be the largest overall purchase you make in your life. Inevitably one discussion you and your spouse will have is the conversation about what your "dream home" would look like. Since hardly anyone pays for cash when they buy a new house, the dream home is going to be acquired through leveraging significant debt. Have you ever noticed on reality TV shows on HGTV that first time property buyers on the search for a new house program almost always pick the highest dollar amount home? Duh! What do you pick? Nice and cozy, fixer upper, or ready to move in today? The important part of this conversation is about expectations of location and then some of the real "must have" elements of the dream home. If you meet someone who has bought a $500,000 or a $1,000,000 home, they'll quickly tell you about all of the rooms they don't use or the fancy gadgets that they never touch. Is the fantabulous kitchen the most important item? Did you always want a walk-in closet? Is it most important to be by the beach? Or the mountains? This discussion is critical to have or you can be very unhappy even if you do reach the pinnacle of getting your dream home?

3. Random spending sprees.

Most people believe if they buy the expensive items that they have always wanted, it will lead to happiness. The truth is that it won't. You may feel a shock of momentary gratification, but wearing that new watch or carrying that ritzy handbag will last like a shot of 5-Hour Energy drink. What you really need to consider is what types of purchases will lead to longer lasting happiness. Perhaps it is a special place your entire family will vacation every year? Or do you and your family really enjoy the theatre or sporting events? If a person buys something in his or her life, they tend to wear the you-know-what out of it. Be careful about making purchases without thinking about long-term happiness it will bring you versus short-term gratification. If you start buying high-end items and your spouse or partner starts matching your purchases, there is an element of disruption that can happen between both of you many years after the fact when you are both climbing your way out of debt. Part of the key here is to manage expectations about how much each of you can spend on special purchases and buying only what will truly make you happy.

If you are struggling as a couple with money issues and it feels like two dogs barking out loud on each side of the table, then start with these questions: What are our expectations of each other when it comes to money? Why are we happy or unhappy at this moment? Is it the person that is making us unhappy, or how we feel about where we are currently relative to where we thought we would be at this time? If you can get explicit with each other about expectations around how money is run in your family, what you will and won't spend money on for purchases, and getting clarity about financial goals, then you will be well on your way to land of happiness.

You Make $100,000 And Live Paycheck To Paycheck

After practicing financial planning for many years, I've found a new financial phenomenon spreading like cancer. There is a growing population of people between the ages of 30 to 50 who make more than $100,000 per year and are literally living paycheck to paycheck. Are these people lacking a college education? No! Are these people lacking a comprehensive set of benefits from their employer? No!

Are these people who are having lots of money garnished from their paychecks every two weeks? No! So how is this group getting so far behind financially while making so much money?

According to a report from the Consumer Federation of America and the Consumer Planner Board of Standards, Inc., over a quarter of households live paycheck-to-paycheck. Many Americans do not even have enough money saved up to weather a financial emergency. In other words, hundreds of millions of people are one mishap away from joining the ranks of the millions of Americans living below the poverty line. All of this speaks to the financial difficulty going on across America, but how are the higher earners facing the same challenges?

PROBLEM #1: No spending plan.
The first problem I see is that many households have never made a spending plan. They worked really hard to get to a six-figure income, and when they finally get to that level they figure it is enough income that they really should be able to buy whatever they want. If they feel like eating out four times a week then it's no problem. A holiday vacation in Costa Rica during the most expensive time of the season . . . then I am worth it. Designer clothes or merchandise on sale . . . then get it while there is a deal. Since there is no measurement system in place holding a six-figure income family in check on how much they spend, unfortunately many of them are spending everything they make. In addition, they can't account for where they spend it when you ask them.

PROBLEM #2: Paying someone else first.
The second problem I see is that most of these people do not have a "pay yourself first" mentality. They have a "pay myself last" mentality. Since there is an internal level of arrogance that there will be a

never-ending supply of jobs that will pay them $100,000 or more because of their skill set, the urgency to put away money for retirement or a rainy day generally falls to the bottom of the pile. These types of earners would be wise to get used to living off of their base income and banking their bonuses. Six figure paycheck-to-paycheck families generally spend their bonus by earmarking it for a discretionary expense before the money even comes into their household.

PROBLEM #3: Refusing to ask for help.
The third problem I see is that the six-figure paycheck-to-paycheck earners feel ashamed to have to ask for professional help. We all know how hard it is to make a $100,000 let alone $300,000 or $400,000 in household income. Earners at this level tell themselves that if they are smart enough and good enough to make this type of income that they should be able to figure out their family finances. How hard could it really be?? The flaw in this logic is that it takes a specific set of skills and expertise to know how to build a family financial plan, balance sheet, and income statement. It is also extremely hard to discipline yourself, which is why many of these people are living paycheck-to-paycheck.

PROBLEM #4: Failing to see the whole financial forest.
The last problem is simply making poor financial decisions without looking at the entire picture. Many six-figure income households will either buy too much home (or too many homes), too pricy an automobile, or not consider the ramifications on items like sending their kids to private school versus public school. By making poor choices around their total financial picture, it puts a tremendous amount of strain on having to earn more versus living comfortably off of the six-figure income.

In a CFP Board Survey, more than twice the percentage of respondents who identified themselves as planners — in comparison to those who admitted to not having a comprehensive financial plan — said they are also living comfortably. This gap between planners and non-planners held true across income brackets — households making just around national median income as well as those earning an excess of $100,000. I believe this trend will continue in America without more families getting back to basics and building a sound financial plan. Do you have little to no debt? Do you have an adequate cash reserve? Are you paying yourself first to reach your financial goals? Are you adequately protected? Or, are you just one paycheck away from wondering where your next paycheck will come from? Make a smart money move and build a plan to turn your six-figure income into a seven figure net worth!

When Should You Replace Your Old Car With A New One?

When it comes to making smart money moves, I've never been a big fan of buying a new car. In fact, the last new car that my wife and I bought was back in 1993 when we really did the math on how much smarter it is to buy a used car that is somewhere between two to four years old versus getting a new one. While getting a new car should be a well thought out and planned purchase, it often falls into the camp of a spur-of-the-moment purchase depending on when you get in the mood. In a sound financial plan, you should begin to save for your next used car purchase the moment that you pay off the old purchase. If you are like us and pay for your cars in cash, you should begin to immediately build a side fund so you can pay for that next automobile purchase in cash as well. So the real question is when is the right time to replace your old car for a new one, especially if you are going to make monthly payments?

The short answer, in my mind, is this: when the cost of upkeep and maintenance on the car becomes more expensive than cost of a payment on a new automobile purchase. Let's breakdown the analysis a little bit further so you can do some analysis on your own. There are more details to look at than you might imagine, so make sure you compare all of these side by side before you take the plunge.

CONSIDERATION #1: Insurance.
The first thing to consider when deciding whether or not to buy a new car is what will happen to the cost of your automobile insurance. With the purchase of a (new) used car, your car insurance is likely to go up. You should call your property and casualty agent or shop around to get a rough idea on what the new cost of your auto insurance will be. Then, you can compare the difference in price between the old car and new car and put the difference in the (new) used car column.

CONSIDERATION #2: Gas.
The second thing to analyze is the cost of gasoline for the purchase. Since your new model may get better or worse mileage depending on choice of automobile, you should make a comparison to see whether gas will cost you more or less money once the new purchase is made. If the style of car will remain the same, then this category may be a push in the overall decision.

CONSIDERATION #3: Maintenance.
The third thing to compare is the cost of overall maintenance. If you are driving a used car into its sixth or seventh year, you may be approaching or already have had it the 100,000-mile mark on the odometer of the car. Depending on the make of the car, it is typically at this level where you could start to see more major repairs. You'll likely have to replace tires, brake pads, or other key parts to the car that can cost you quite a few bucks. You may want to look back at your credit

cards to see how much you actually spent in overall major maintenance costs is the past few years. Even if the car is bought with some
sort of extended warranty, you may still have some out of pocket cost
for upkeep and maintenance, but you'll need to factor this in for the
side-by-side comparison. Items like oil changes should stay relatively
the same if you change your oil every 3,000 to 5,000 miles.

CONSIDERATION #4: Safety.
The fourth thing to compare is overall safety of the automobile. This
part of the equation may be very difficult to measure when it comes to
dollars and cents, but could factor into the decision when it comes to
your automobile insurance rates or your overall peace of mind. Safety
can be even more important to your decision if you have added a new
addition to the family since the last time you purchased a new car.

CONSIDERATION #5: Payment.
The last part of the analysis is to determine what the monthly payment will be on the (new) used car. You should always make sure
you negotiate with the car dealer on the price of the car and never
start your negotiation with amount of payment you can afford each
month. After you determine what you can afford for a down payment, you should be able to determine the cost of your payment at
different borrowing rates. Often you can get great rates from places
like your local credit union if the dealer does not offer you a good
interest rate on the loan.

Purchasing a vehicle can be a very emotional process for most
households. Considering the size of this purchase and what it will
mean to your overall budget, you should absolutely make a smart
money move and do a detailed T-chart side-by-side analysis so you
can make the best decision for your family.

Should You Rent The House Or Sell It?

One of the tough questions that many newly married couples face is what to do with the real estate properties they own when they get married. It's almost a certainty that if both of you own a home, you'll end up moving into one of your properties as a couple. This begs the questions of what will happen to the remaining piece of real estate once the movers have packed the boxes and the house is empty. Newly married couples often grapple with the challenge on whether to rent the empty property and keep it as a rental property or just move on and sell the property to get whatever equity is available. With a great deal of homes still underwater in value, here are some smart money moves to consider when you make this big decision.

QUESTION #1: Do you want to be a landlord?

Keeping a rental property can be advantageous to your long-term investment plans if you are consistent in keeping a quality renter in the property without damaging your property at all. Even if your cash flow is neutral after paying all of your bills, you have the long-term potential of having someone else pay off the mortgage on your rental property. This means at some point you will have a debt-free asset to sell or an income-producing asset to keep in retirement. However, if you run into a situation where you have bad renters or cannot find a consistent tenant to pay rent, you run the risk of negative cash flow, which can be a drain on your family finances.

QUESTION #2: What kind of upkeep will the house need?

Remember that if you cannot be cash flow positive, the property will ultimately need some level of upkeep. Many people use this rule-of-thumb: your home will on an annual basis need somewhere between 1% to 2% of the overall value of the house for ongoing maintenance and upkeep. This means if your rental property is $200,000, you'll need a side cash fund of $2,000 to $4,000 in case you need a new water heater, air conditioning units, or something else that may go in the house. Most people who own rental properties do not plan for these types of emergencies that may come up over the course of the year.

QUESTION #3: Is there equity in the house?

Real estate in general is a long-term asset class to hold. You generally shouldn't buy real estate unless you have 5 years or more to hold the property and in today's market it may be more like 10 years. There are experts who know how to property flip, but the odds are it isn't you. If your spouse's property is underwater, it may make sense to hold on to the house for several years to see if you can get a rebound in the value of the home rather than try to short sell it which can damage your credit as a newly married couple. If the property has equity in the house, consider the overall trajectory of growth of the value of the house compared to the cash you have in your hand to invest in other ideas.

QUESTION #4: Can you refinance?

You may have looked into this option already, but one of the questions before you turn it into a rental property is to see whether you can refinance. Typically, rates are a little bit higher on rental properties than on your primary residence. With rates around all time lows, you should check into a refinance to see if you can lower your overall costs before you explore the idea of renting.

QUESTION #5: Can you actually rent the house?

One of the very important items to do some research on before you consider selling or renting is to see if you are even eligible to rent. It is possible that your homeowner's or condo association only allows for a certain amount of homes or condominium units to be rented out within the development or building. Renting may not even be an option, which could force your hand toward other alternatives.

QUESTION #6: Will you get any additional tax break?

You should check with your Certified Public Accountant on this one, but depending on your overall adjusted gross income and how the property is structured, you may or may not be eligible for a tax break. Most people will use straight-line depreciation on the property over the life of the property, so you may run into a situation where you are cash flow neutral and actually have a tax loss on paper. This is a critical piece of the equation when you start looking at the math.

The Clash wrote and performed a track called, "Should I Stay or Should I Go?" You should consider making a smart money move and enlisting a financial advisor, CPA, or a top real estate agent to discuss these important money decisions before you decide to lean one way or another. You'll have a lot going on as a newly married couple just by deciding whose house you will live in when you get married. Renting or selling that empty property can be one of the first difficult decisions as a couple, so make sure you do your own inspection with pros and cons so you can make the right call.

Is An Equity Indexed Annuity A Good Idea?

With all of the ups and downs in the stock market, many investors have been asking this question, "Is there a way to make money in the stock market and still have a way not to lose my principal if the market goes down?" While investment companies have scrambled to find different investment solutions to help the baby boomers with this particular issue, the sales of a product called an equity-indexed annuity have been booming. An equity-indexed annuity is an annuity that earns interest that is linked to a stock or other equity index. One of the most commonly used indices is the Standard & Poor's 500 Composite Stock Price Index (the S&P 500). It can be a very complex choice on whether to purchase one of these products in your portfolio.

Source: www.finra.org

What is an Annuity? An annuity is a contract between you and an insurance company in which the company promises to make periodic payments to you, starting immediately or at some future time. If the payments are delayed to the future, you have a deferred annuity. If the payments start immediately, you have an immediate annuity. You buy the annuity either with a single payment or a series of payments called premiums. Annuities come in two types: fixed and variable. With a fixed annuity, the insurance company guarantees both the rate of return and the payout. As its name implies, a variable annuity's rate of return is not stable, but varies with the performance of the stock, bond and money market investment options that you choose. There is no guarantee that you will earn any return on your investment and there is a risk that you will lose money. Unlike fixed contracts, variable annuities are securities registered with the Securities and Exchange Commission (SEC).

What is an Equity-Indexed Annuity?

EIAs are complex financial instruments that have characteristics of both fixed and variable annuities. Their return varies more than a fixed annuity, but not as much as a variable annuity. So EIAs give you more risk (but more potential return) than a fixed annuity but less risk (and less potential return) than a variable annuity. EIAs offer a minimum guaranteed interest rate combined with an interest rate linked to a market index. Because of the guaranteed interest rate, EIAs have less market risk than variable annuities. EIAs also have the potential to earn returns better than traditional fixed annuities when the stock market is rising.

What is the Guaranteed Minimum Return?

When EIAs were first sold in the mid-1990s, the guaranteed minimum return was typically 90 percent of the premium paid at a 3 percent annual interest rate. More recently, in part because of changes to state insurance laws, the guaranteed minimum return is typically at least 87.5 percent of the premium paid at 1 to 3 percent interest. However, if you surrender your EIA early, you may have to pay a significant surrender charge and a 10 percent tax penalty that will reduce or eliminate any return.

How good is this guarantee?

Your guaranteed return is only as good as the insurance company that gives it. While it is not a common occurrence that a life insurance company is unable to meet its obligations, it happens. There are several private companies that rate an insurance company's financial strength. Information about these firms can be found on the SEC's website.

What is a Market Index?

A Market Index tracks the performance of a specific group of stocks representing a particular segment of the market, or in some cases an entire market. For example, the S&P 500 Composite Stock Price Index is an index of 500 stocks intended to be a representative of a broad segment of the market. There are indexes for almost every conceivable sector of the stock market. Most EIAs are based on the S&P 500, but other indexes also are used. Some EIAs even allow investors to select one or more indexes.

How is an EIA's index-linked interest rate computed?

The index-linked gain depends on the particular combination of indexing features that an EIA uses. The most common indexing features are listed below. To fully understand an EIA, make sure you not only understand each feature, but also how the features work together since these features can dramatically impact the return on your investment.

• **Participation Rates.** A participation rate determines how much of the gain in the index will be credited to the annuity. For example, the insurance company may set the participation rate at 80 percent, which means the annuity would only be credited with 80 percent of the gain experienced by the index.

• **Spread/Margin/Asset Fee.** Some EIAs use a spread, margin or asset fee in addition to, or instead of, a participation rate. This percentage will be subtracted from any gain in the index linked to the annuity. For example, if the index gained 10 percent and the spread/margin/asset fee is 3.5 percent, then the gain in the annuity would be only 6.5 percent.

• **Interest Rate Caps.** Some EIAs may put a cap or upper limit on your return. This cap rate is generally stated as a percentage. This is the maximum rate of interest the annuity will earn. For example, if the index linked to the annuity gained 10 percent and the cap rate was 8 percent, then the gain in the annuity would be 8 percent.

Caution! Some EIA's allow the insurance company to change partici- pation rates, cap rates, or spread/asset/margin fees either annually or at the start of the next contract term. If an insurance company subsequently lowers the participation rate or cap rate or increas- es the spread/asset/margin fees, this could adversely affect your return. Read your contract carefully to see if it allows the insurance company to change these features.

What are the basic Indexing Methods? As described in the table below, there are several methods for determining the change in the relevant index over the period of the annuity. These varying methods impact the calculation of the amount of interest to be credited to the contract based on a change in the index.

Indexing Method	Description
Annual Reset (Rachet)	Compares the change in the index from the beginning to the end of each year. Any declines are ignored. Advantage: Your gain is "locked in" each year. Disadvantage: Can be combined with other features, such as lower cap rates and participation rates that will limit the amount of interest you might gain each year.
High Water Mark	Looks at the index value at various points during the contract, usually annual anniversaries. It then takes the highest of these values and compares it to the index level at the start of the term. Advantage: May credit you with more interest than other indexing methods and protect against declines in the index. Disadvantage: Because interest is not credited until the end of the term, you may not receive any index-link gain if you surrender your EIA early. It can also be combined with other features; such as lower cap rates and participation rates that will limit the amount of interest you might gain each year.

Indexing Method	Description
Point-to-Point	Compares the change in the index at two discrete points in time, such as the beginning and ending dates of the contract term. Advantage: May be combined with other features, such as higher cap and participation rates, that may credit you with more interest. Disadvantage: Relies on single point in time to calculate interest. Therefore, even if the index that your annuity is linked to is going up throughout the term of your investment, if it declines dramatically on the last day of the term, then part or all of the earlier gain can be lost. Because interest is not credited until the end of the term, you may not receive any index-link gain if you surrender your EIA early.

Other terms:

Index Averaging: Some EIAs average an index's value either daily or monthly rather than use the actual value of the index on a specified date. Averaging may reduce the amount of index-linked interest you earn.

Interest Calculation: The way that an insurance company calculates interest earned during the term of an EIA can make a big difference in the amount of money you will earn. Some EIAs pay simple interest during the term of the annuity. Because there is no compounding of interest, your return will be lower.

Exclusion of Dividends: Most EIAs only count equity index gains from market price changes, excluding any gains from dividends. Since you're not earning dividends, you won't earn as much as if you invested directly in the market.

Can you get money when you need it?

EIAs are long-term investments. Getting out early may mean taking a loss. Many EIAs have surrender charges. The surrender charge can be a percentage of the amount withdrawn or a reduction in the interest rate credited to the EIA. Also, any withdrawals from tax-deferred annuities before you reach the age of 59½ are generally subject to a 10 percent tax penalty in addition to any gain being taxed as ordinary income.

Do EIAs and other tax-deferred annuities provide the same advantages as 401(k)s and other before tax retirement plans?

No, 401(k) plans and other before-tax retirement savings plans not only allow you to defer taxes on income and investment gains, but your contributions reduce your current taxable income. That's why most investors should consider an EIA and other annuity products only after they make the maximum contribution to their 401(k) and other before-tax retirement plans. To learn more about 401(k)s, please read "Smart 401(k) Investing" on FINRA's website.

Is it possible to lose money in an EIA?

Yes. Many insurance companies only guarantee that you'll receive 87.5 percent of the premiums you paid, plus 1 to 3 percent interest. Therefore, if you don't receive any index-linked interest, you could lose money on your investment. One way that you could not receive any index-linked interest is if the index linked to your annuity declines. The other way you may not receive any index-linked interest is if you surrender your EIA before maturity. Some insurance companies will not credit you with index-linked interest when you surrender your annuity early.

Source: www.finra.org

How Much Should You Give For A Wedding Gift?

Your college roommate or long time childhood friend invites you to their wedding. Or better yet, you've got a big family and your second cousin Joe is getting married and last time you saw him was two years ago at the family reunion. Now you have got to spend money to get an airline ticket, block a hotel room, and possibly buy a new dress or suit for the upcoming wedding this summer. It dawns on you that now you've got to figure out how much is the right amount to give for a wedding gift. You are no Miss Manners by any stretch of the imagination, but you don't want to walk away like some cheapskate that the wedding couple laughs at that evening when they open up their gifts. So, how much should you give for a wedding gift?

Everyone has different thoughts on this, but let's talk first if you can't attend the wedding. By no means should you consider a wedding invitation as a personal invoice for you to spend money. If you don't attend the wedding and it's someone close and personal to you, sending some type of gift (not cash) or something off of the couple's engagement registry should suffice. Getting a wedding invitation can certainly play tricks on your mind when it comes to making the right financial decisions if you cannot attend a wedding. Don't feel like the invitation is a measure of extortion for you to turn your wallet upside down if you don't attend. Make a gesture that makes sense if you are close the couple, and if you aren't don't feel bad if you don't do something more than a small gift from their registry.

The real challenge begins weighing out your total financial decision about the money you have to invest getting or going to the wedding. I've always stuck to a very simple rule: that you should try to cover your plate. Sometimes, we don't know if our plate costs $50 or $250, but you should use your best judgment based upon the location and what you may know about the size of the wedding. There are many articles on etiquette that you don't have to worry about covering your dinner and just do what's affordable in your budget. You don't want to spend money you don't have to make the bride and groom happy, but let's be honest: if you give them a Wok from Wal-Mart they probably won't use it.

If it is a destination wedding or your travel costs take you far away you can consider this in your overall gift especially if it is a close friend that really wants to see you. Destination wedding couples generally don't want gifts, as they know the cost associated with you (and your guest) traveling to the wedding.

Most etiquette sites, like FabAndFru.com say the following, "Think of it this way: the cost of the gift does not equal the price of admission into the party. The wedding gift should be thought of as more of a gesture that commemorates and helps the couple start their new life together." I think it makes sense to do your very best to give a gift (or a gift card) that would cover your plate for the wedding.

The debate around this will probably go on for many years to come about what the "right thing to do" is when it comes to gift giving at the next wedding you attend. At the end of day, come up with a rule that makes sense to you so you don't have to spend a lot of time internally debating what you are "supposed to do."

Chapter 2

Dealing with Debt

Debt. That four-letter word can simultaneously make us look like Rockefellers while, in reality, living from paycheck to paycheck. In this chapter, we are going to dig into debt – in a good way. You learn how to understand debt, how to get rid of it, and how to use credit cards wisely. I believe that the key to a successful financial future is having zero debt – being debt free will in the long run allow you to do more the things you want to do. So, let's tackle debt and get you on the road to having a life where you can make your money work for you, versus working to pay off your debt.

Here's Why Your Friends Are Going Broke

Most of the time when we talk about personal finance, topics including credit card debt, savings, investments, insurance, and coupons creep into the discussion. Since nobody wears their net worth pinned to their chest, we truly have no inkling what our neighbors' real personal financial situation is at any given point and time. What is true is that what appears to be an ocean of success around you is merely nothing more than a mirage of many people living on an obligatory basis to pay their bills. Your friends will never tell you they are drowning in debt, but people around you are going broke every day. Here are the reasons why.

1. Ego

Your ego is something that can make you stronger or it can become an insurmountable obstacle to achieving success. Remember, your ego is the part of your mind that contains memory. It is ultimately what shapes your planning and your reality. When it comes to money, ego is one of those drivers that make people you know broke. This doesn't mean that they are living out in a trailer park, but it does mean that they are fulfilled by keeping up with the Jones and eating out at the latest and greatest restaurant. How will your ego react when your neighbor buys a new Range Rover? Or puts in a new pool in their backyard? Or takes a 10 day vacation come Christmas time in the British Virgin Islands?

2. Irrationality.

A great book, *Predictably Irrational* by Dan Ariely, has some fascinating stories. But the truth is that most of your friends make irrational decisions around their money in spite of the facts in front of them. For instance, some people don't take advantage of the free match from their employer as a part of the company-sponsored 401(k) because they don't believe they can save money. We are talking about FREE money! Another problem: People don't take gains in their investments after a great run because they believe their portfolio will go up forever. It's similar to being at the black jack table and thinking you can beat the dealer forever. Sadly, people convince themselves to buy a swimming pool telling their brain that the value of their house will go up when all other statistics suggest otherwise.

3. Education.

In my opinion, time is now the #1 money killer in today's society. There is so much information coming at the average consumer that it's difficult to decipher fact from fiction. People you know who are broke (or going broke) are too ashamed to ask for help because they went to a top-ranked college and/or have a graduate degree. They assume a quick search on Google will help them get all of the information they need. However, both purchasing decisions and investment decisions have become more complex. Benefits at work are more difficult to understand. Credit card contracts require you to read the fine print. Just because you are college educated doesn't mean you are financially educated. In fact, when was the last time you took a serious personal finance course?

The reality behind all of this is that knowing and doing are two very different concepts. We all know we need to lose weight, yet without a program most people fail. We all know we need to exercise, yet without a weekly regimen most of us get off track. If you meet someone in their 40's or early 50's and ask them what their biggest worry is in life, they won't say their health; instead they'll say "money." If that's the case, then why are so many people going broke and living just to meet the standard of life that they have built for themselves? Ask your friends… that is if they are willing to put their ego on the table!

What Every Student Needs To Know About Student Loans After They Graduate

Shortly after graduation, many college graduates begin embarking on their first job in the "official" workforce. According to USA Today, student loan debt has increased a whopping 84% since the 2008 recession and has now exceeded more than $1.2 trillion. With the average student debt payment around $280 a month, here are some things all students should know about living life with student loans after they graduate.

1. Know the grace period.
The grace period refers to the amount of time you can wait for repayment although I suggest that you can start repaying automatically in order to alleviate a little bit of interest owed. Depending on the kind of loan(s) you have, the grace period will vary. You'll have a six-

month grace period on Stafford Loans, while Federal Perkins Loans allow a nine-month grace period. Other loans, like PLUS loans, vary from loan to loan.

2. Understand your loans.

The first, and most important step is to understand everything you van about your loan(s). A good starting point is the National Student Loan Data System (www.nslds.ed.gov), which is a central place to look at all of your loans. You will want to figure out how much you own and track down any and all private loans you have and compile one master loan spreadsheet, Pay particular attention to your interest rates, if they are too high, you may want to consider refinancing your loans.

3. Build a repayment plan strategy.

Nowadays, student loan debt payments are designed to be paid off in 10 years. You should review the difference between income driven repayment plans to see what monthly payment you need to be making. These plans can include income- based repayment (IBR) or pay as you earn (PAYE). Each of these plans takes into account how much money you are currently making in order to ensure that you can live with your student loan debt. Lastly, you might be able to have debt forgiven after 10 years if you work for certain government agencies or certain.

4. Stay out of trouble.

Student loan debt can certainly give you the blues. However, you want to make sure that if you are ever in financial trouble and cannot pay your student loan debt, speak with your loan service provider. If at all possible, you want to avoid defaulting on your student loans. Default can happen after 9 months of non-payment and can negatively affect your credit score, which will impact many parts of your financial life. You are unable to discharge student loan debt in a bankruptcy and the government can garnish your wages or tax refunds to pay student loan debt.

Debt can take both a financial and emotional toll on a new college graduate. It's best to sit down now and begin to build out a budget and an initial financial game plan for your future.

10 Ways To Reduce Your Credit Card Debt

Those that end up bing wealthy make it a habit NOT to carry debt on their credit cards. If you have a goal this year to get rid of your credit card debt (and you should), here are 10 ideas to help you get rid of the plastic hangover.

1. Pay off the credit card with the lowest balance.

Even though some credit cards may have a higher balance, putting a check mark in the win column by paying off just one credit card will get you fired up to pay off another.

2. Pay cash for three months.

If you walk into a grocery store or a department store with cash, you can only get as far as your wallet will take you. By physically not using a credit card for three months, your habits and how you think about money will begin to change.

3. Switch your credit card debt to a lower rate.

If you can qualify for a zero balance credit card transfer or some type of low introductory rate, this can help you slow down the bleeding while you pay off your debt. There are many good websites to help you compare credit cards. Try www.billshrink.com as a starter.

4. Get down to two or three credit cards.

You really don't need store cards for any good reason, and if you get down to two or three major brand credit cards that should be enough if you actually need a card. If you are paying off your bills, I recommend getting a card that will give you some type of rewards program.

5. Get rid of a vice or guilty splurge.

Debt is often built up by our guilty pleasures whether they are large or small ones. Just pick one vice you can get rid of for a year whether it is the fancy morning coffee, twice-a-month manicures, wine or cigarettes. This will put some much-needed money in your pocket and off the card.

6. Earn additional income.

Whether it is a small part-time business or just an extra day of work on the weekend, working to earn additional income that you use to pay down your debt is a good use of time.

7. Make your payments on time.

Credit card companies thrive on the fact that you just won't pay your bills promptly, thus whacking you with late fees and charges. Just make sure you have your online bill pay set to the right day or mail your check early enough to avoid these costly fees.

8. Delay your gratification.

Implement a 48-hour rule. If you are going to make a major purchase, just wait 48 hours before you buy it to be certain that you need it. If you put this rule into effect, you will find yourself making less impulse purchases, and really begin questioning what you really have to buy to make ends meet.

9. Talk to your spouse/partner.

If you are in a spender/saver relationship and your partner is the spender, have an honest conversation around how many credit cards you both have. There is nothing more damaging in a relationship than having hidden money and debt that the other partner doesn't know about lurking around the corner.

10. Change your lifestyle.

Let's face it: most people live beyond their means. Everyone wants a little taste of the good life and what we see on television. However, most of us can live very well without having the luxury brand of everything. Consider how important those items are when they bring the everyday stress of carrying credit card debt. Do you really need those items that badly?

The Financial Ghost Of Spending Past

There is nothing more haunting than dwelling on the bad decisions we have made in our lives. For one reason or another our brain tends to drift positive or negative and, more often than not, most of us tend to dwell on the things that haven't gone well versus the things that have. Now is a fantastic time to consider financial decisions that have gone wrong or prevented you from moving forward, and make the necessary adjustments to improve your financial future. Here are ten things to consider.

1. Investing in things you don't understand.

You've done it before, now stop it. If you can't explain it, don't bother putting your money it.

2. Investing in a friend's business.

If you aren't running it, don't put money in it. Nine out of ten times, you'll lose all of your money.

3. Buying too large a home.
Count the number of rooms in your current home you don't use. If it was more than one, you've made a mistake.

4. Buying a new car.
As I discussed in Chapter One, the best way to lose your money quickly is when you buy a car that costs more than $50,000 – not to mention the upkeep. Stick to a two-year old car.

5. Forgetting to increase savings.
When you make more money, unless you put it away automatically, the spending gods will get it. Have some sort of money ACH or Bank-o-Matic set up each month. Get it out of your hands and into your savings account.

6. Set vacation budgets.
Every vacation doesn't have to be at a 4- or 5-star hotel. A few nice memories of vacations are important, but if you are spending $10,000 or more a year on vacations there might be a problem.

7. Trusting your company.
Large companies have a heart smaller than the Grinch. Make sure you have alternative plans set up at all times just case you need to exit stage left.

8. Having too much in company stock.
Ask anybody who saw the technology bubble burst in 2000 about the effects of having too much of your money invested in company stock. Unfortunately, people have a really short memory and may have forgotten the havoc that wreaked on investment portfolios. Make sure to get some of your cash off the table (out of your company's stock) every year.

9. Sticking with the wrong partner.

You must get synced up financially as family. Spender vs. Saver relationships are difficult for making progress unless you have a plan. If you are both Spenders, then getting a financial coach will be the best investment you have ever made. You must work as a team.

10. Debt (Period)!

Do you want two tons of bricks sitting on your shoulders? That's what debt can feel like. I know a lot of financial advisors who say that your money can do better than your debt. But, when you factor in how debt makes you feel emotionally, it is often better to rid yourself of debt. I love having no debt!

To get yourself fiscally fit, you do have to revisit the financial ghosts of your past. Don't be embarrassed or ashamed because we have all made financial mistakes. Just don't make them twice!

How To Pick A Credit Card

A credit card can be a useful tool or it can be a dangerous weapon. Most of this depends on you — the best credit card in the world won't help if you spend beyond your means. American adults carry thousands of dollars in credit card debt. This is not something anyone wants to live with and I don't recommend it. If you're responsible, a credit card can be both convenient and efficient. For example, I save 1% on my utilities by paying with my cash-back credit card. These are expenditures I'd make anyway, but the card saves me money. (As a bonus, using the credit card helps with my quest for a paperless personal finance system.) But there are hundreds (thousands?) of different credit cards to choose from, and you can compare each card against the average credit card rates, but beyond that how can you tell which is best?

When asked for credit card recommendations in the past, I've always declined. First, *I'm still not completely convinced that credit cards are a good idea.* Second, I don't have the resources to judge which cards are best. I do know, however, know that it's important to choose the right card for your lifestyle. Here are a few tips:

- *If you are someone who carries credit card debt, focus on cards that offer low interest rates (especially on balance transfers) — and put a stop to new charges.*
- *If you pay your balance in full every month, find a cash back credit card with no annual fees and/or solid cash rewards program.*
- *Some credit card users have special needs. If you spend a lot on gas, consider a gas credit card that gives added rewards on auto expenses. If you travel a lot, look for a card with rewards for flights and lodging.*

When choosing a credit card, *Money* magazine recommends you pay special attention to the Schumer Box, a prominent table in every credit card application. In general it's important that you understand the different aspects of the credit card application. Look for:

- *An annual percentage rate that is 11% or less on purchases.*
- *Low rates on other loans, such as cash advances or balance transfers. (If you're doing a balance transfer, find a card that offers 0% APR for at least a year.)*
- *Reasonable penalty terms. Find the penalty rate (or default rate), and follow the asterisk to see what triggers it.*
- *Finance charges that are not computed using two-cycle billing. (Two-cycle billing stinks.)*
- *No annual fee.*

Don't choose a card just because it offers a signup bonus or because it gives you a discount at your favorite store.
Read the terms and conditions. Understand the card's limitations. Remember: your goal is to pick a tool, like a vacuum cleaner. You're not looking for a one-time bonus, but a long-term relationship you can live with.

When your credit card plans to increase your rate or other fees, they must send you a notice 45 days before they can increase your interest rate; change certain fees (such as annual fees, cash advance fees, and late fees) that apply to your account; or make other significant changes to the terms of your card.

If your credit card company is going to make changes to the terms of your card, it must give you the option to cancel the card before certain fee increases take effect. If you take that option, however, your credit card company may close your account and increase your monthly payment, subject to certain limitations. For example, they can require you to pay the balance off in five years, or they can double the percentage of your balance used to calculate your minimum payment (which will result in faster repayment than under the terms of your account).

The caveat here is that the company does **not** have to send you a 45-day advance notice if you have a variable interest rate tied to an index; if the index goes up, the company does not have to provide notice before your rate goes up; your introductory rate expires and reverts to the previously disclosed "go-to" rate; your rate increases because you are in a workout agreement and you haven't made your payments as agreed.

Your monthly credit card bill will also include information on how long it will take you to pay off your balance if you only make minimum payments. It will also tell you how much you would need to pay each month in order to pay off your balance in three years. For example, suppose you owe $3,000 and your interest rate is 14.4% – your bill might look like this:

New Balance	$3,000.00
Minimum payment due	$90.00
Payment due date	4/20/12

Late Payment Warning. If we do not receive your minimum payment by the date listed above, you may have to pay a $35 late fee and your APRs may be increased up to the Penalty APR of 28.99%.

Minimum Payment Warning. If you make only the minimum payment each period, you will pay more in interest and it will take you longer to pay off your balance. For example:

If you make no additional charges using this card and each month you pay...	You will pay off the balance shown on this statement in about...	And you will end up paying an estimated total of. . .
Only the minimum payment	11 years	$4,745
$103	3 years	$3,712 (Savings = $1,033)

You should also be aware of these rules regarding rates, fees, and limits:

No interest rate increases for the first year.
Your credit card company cannot increase your rate for the first twelve months after you open an account. There are some exceptions:

- *If your card has a variable interest rate tied to an index; your rate can go up whenever the index goes up.*
- *If there is an introductory rate, it must be in place for at least six months; after that your rate can revert to the "go-to" rate the company disclosed when you got the card.*
- *If you are more than sixty days late in paying your bill, your rate can go up.*
- *If you are in a workout agreement and you don't make your payments as agreed, your rate can go up.*

Increased rates apply only to new charges. If your credit card company does raise your interest rate after the first year, the new rate will apply only to new charges you make. If you have a balance, your old interest rate will apply to that balance.

Restrictions on over-the-limit transactions. You must tell your credit card company that you want it to allow transactions that will take you over your credit limit. Otherwise, if a transaction would take you over your limit, it may be turned down. If you do not opt-in to over-the-limit transactions and your credit card company allows one to go through, it cannot charge you an over-the-limit fee. If you opt-in to allowing transactions that take you over your credit limit, your credit card company can impose only one fee per billing cycle. You can revoke your opt-in at any time.

Caps on high-fee cards. If your credit card company requires you to pay fees (such as an annual fee or application fee), those fees cannot total more than 25% of the initial credit limit. For example, if your initial credit limit is $500, the fees for the first year cannot be more than $125. This limit does not apply to penalty fees, such as penalties for late payments.

Protections for underage consumers. If you are under 21, you will need to show that you are able to make payments, or you will need a cosigner, in order to open a credit card account. If you are under age 21 and have a card with a cosigner and want an increase in the credit limit, your cosigner must agree in writing to the increase.

Standard payment dates and times. Your credit card company must mail or deliver your credit card bill at least 21 days before your payment is due. In addition:

- *Your due date should be the same date each month (for example, your payment is always due on the 15th or always due on the last day of the month).*
- *The payment cut-off time cannot be earlier than 5 p.m. on the due date.*
- *If your payment due date is on a weekend or holiday (when the company does not process payments), you will have until the following business day to pay. (For example, if the due date is Sunday the 15th, your payment will be on time if it is received by Monday the 16th before 5 p.m.).*

Payments directed to highest interest balances first. If you make more than the minimum payment on your credit card bill, your credit card company must apply the excess amount to the balance with the highest interest rate. There is an exception:

- *If you made a purchase under a deferred interest plan (for example, "no interest if paid in full by March 2012"), the credit card company may let you choose to apply extra amounts to the deferred interest balance before other balances. Otherwise, for two billing cycles prior to the end of the deferred interest period, the credit card company must apply your entire payment to the deferred interest-rate balance first.*

No two-cycle (double-cycle) billing. Credit card companies can only impose interest charges on balances in the current billing cycle.

Tips on selecting and activating a credit card

Look for a card that has good benefits. Good benefits may include low interest, promotional interest rates, no annual fee, no bank service charges, air travel bonus miles, credit points toward purchases, credit points toward long-distance phone calls, or credit points for gasoline. Compare Credit Cards with 0% APR at www.compare-cards.com

If offered a promotional interest rate, find out the terms of payment and when the rate will expire. Most cards apply payments to lowest interest charges first, leaving your higher interest charges to collect interest until the entire amount is paid off.

Ask if there are fees and charges. There may be an annual fee, an application fee, an account service charge, an over-limit fee, a late-payment fee, a cash advance fee, and other miscellaneous fees. Compare these fees to other cards to see if they are trying to rip you off.

Check the interest rates. Some cards charge interest from the date of purchase. Some cards charge interest from the billing date. Pay all of your bills on time to avoid paying interest.

Find out if the card offers a standard monthly billing cycle. Some cards expect a payment every two weeks! Ask if there is a penalty for not using your card.

Apply. There are usually three ways to apply: through the mail, over the phone and on the Internet.

Activate the card when you receive it. Follow the activation instructions included with the card; usually this can only be done from your home phone. They will try to sell you several services over the phone. Say no. Sign the back of the card before you use it.

Three Ways Credit Card Companies Can Trick You

When the Dodd-Frank Wall Street Reform and Consumer Protection Act was put into place, credit card holders were supposed to benefit from the new regulation. Under the Act, consumers would receive new notifications for rate fee increases, statements would inform consumers on how long it would take to pay off balances, and credit issuers were required to mail bills at least 21 days before the due date. Now that some time has passed since the passage of the Dodd-Frank Act, consumers are still struggling with all-time high levels of credit card debt and the fine print coming from credit card companies are smaller than ever. Here are three things you should keep an eye on so you don't get stung by the credit card companies.

1. Late fees.

Late fees are a big source of credit card company's earnings. Make sure you pay your credit card bill a few days before the actual due date. Some credit card companies will give their customers several weeks to pay their bill before late fees or finance charges will be incurred. However, some credit card companies will begin charging late fees and finance charges literally the next day after the due date.

You need to read the fine print on your credit card statements and fulfillments you get from them because they may change their policies and actually move the dates around.

2. Introductory annual percentage rate.

I'm sure you see television and Internet advertisements that entice us to open a new credit card with a 0% introductory rate. There are also mailings that will allow us to transfer our balances over to a new credit card with a 0% interest rate on the balance transfer. If you are going to do a balance transfer to a 0% card, be sure you closely read the fine print on what happens with new purchases or cash advances. Often, the card issuers that give you this 0% rate will charge the maximum possible interest rate on new purchases or new cash advances. It is very important to decide in advance whether you will need the card you transfer the balance to for floating new credit. If you take a new credit card with an introductory 0% rate, then be sure to read the fine print on how long the rate will last, what types of purchases it covers, and what the interest rate will be once the introductory rate expires.

3. Inactivity or annual fees.

Since credit is at a premium today, you need to manage your credit cards more closely than ever. If you are inactive with the credit cards that you have, it is likely that the credit card companies will shrink your overall credit limit. Some of the credit card companies will get sneaky and can actually charge you an inactivity fee if you are not careful or do not spend a certain amount on the card. This is true with many new offers sent to consumers today. In addition, you should be clear when you sign up what the annual fees will be. Some cards offer more rewards, benefits, and features that will make the annual fee worthwhile. However, some cards will charge excessive fees without any real particular benefit.

Credit card companies are businesses. We all know this. Yet, it is only when we open our statements and see extra charges and fees that we get into a fit of rage with a customer service person that really is less than interested in our diatribe or empowered to really help us. Make sure you limit the number of credit cards you have in your wallet and read each piece of new mail you get from your credit card company as they send them to share important information with you. Don't get caught with your credit card company sneaking into your wallet!

Where to Get An Unsecured Line Of Credit

In the past five or six years, for many Americans it probably feels like the world of getting a line of credit parallels being at a David Copperfield magic show. At one time, you could easily get one or two free offers in the mail to consolidate your debt or gain access to easy capital, but the days of capturing an unsecured line of credit have all but vanished within our banking system. It's hard enough to acquire new capital if you are a small business owner as you practically have to give your left arm, right eye, and personally guarantee everything you own just to get some funds into your hands. Even worse, if you are an individual with a small amount of personal debt you need to clean up in the range of $5,000 to $25,000, going straight down to your local bank to get these funds can be nearly impossible.

However, for both investors and debtors alike, every time there is a serious problem it will create the potential for a tremendous opportunity. Over the past several years, Americans in need of credit have relied on friends, family members, and even work colleagues to borrow money in a pinch. On the Internet today, the scarcity of loans from "traditional" sources and the increasing level of debt has generated a thriving market in microloans. If you have to get your hands on some short-term cash to pay off a car loan, consolidate credit card debt, or even do an addition to your home, here are some websites that may be able to fill the void in your financial life.

1. Lending Club (www.lendingclub.com).

Lending club is a website that brings together both investors and debtors who are interested in dealing with unsecured personal loans. With Lending Club, you can attain a loan for three or five years for automobiles, credit cards, home improvement, and even special events. Based upon a number of factors including your personal credit score, you will receive a ranking from A to F, which will ultimately dictate your overall interest rate. Lending Club will link your bank account for repayment of the loans so the payment comes out automatically. There is no charge for early repayment of the loan. Here's the catch: You can only get the funding by attracting investors out there that want to invest in your debt. So, if you are looking to get your hands on $10,000 in funds, it could take 100 or 200 different investors before your loan is funded.

2. Prosper (www.prosper.com).

Prosper is another microloan website created to incent peer-to-peer lending. Simply put, Prosper wants to connect people who want to invest money with those out there who want to borrow money. Similar to Lending Club, Prosper will offer three to five year terms on loans that range from $2,000 to $35,000. Your identity is never shown to people who invest in your overall debt, but your rate will be determined on your "Prosper Rating," which is generally based on your Experian credit score . Be careful about interest rates, because lower rated debtors can pay over 35% interest on their money.

3. Lending Tree (www.lendingtree.com).

Lending Tree became one of the more popular websites by advertising their tool that allows comparison of three or four different mortgage brokers for a home loan. While mortgages have been their bread and butter, Lending Tree also offers credit avenues such as auto loans and unsecured loans called signature loans for credit card debt and even payday advances. The main issue with Lending Tree, like any other bank out there, is that the process for getting approved is difficult. Those with a higher credit score will have a really good opportunity to be able to secure some capital while those at the lower end won't stand much chance of acquiring a loan.

It's fascinating to see how companies evolve and financial opportunities become available as shifting market and economic conditions change. If you are in a pinch to get capital and are having a hard time with a bank, websites like Prosper, Lending Tree, and Lending Club can all provide opportunities to solve your problem. Remember, that carrying any type of unsecured debt is generally not a good idea, but using one of these sites could be a Smart Money Move to get some cash without having to sign away your life!

Should You Refinance Your Mortgage?

Whenever interest rates are low, the question always becomes whether or not you should refinance your mortgage. Sometimes those that did refinance, even 18 months ago, may be licking their chops to do the tango again soon. Mortgage rates have been at historic lows, and the rates are even better in the jumbo market – those mortgages above $417,000. However, if you do not need a jumbo mortgage, here are some things to help you decide whether a refinance is right for you.

1. How long will you live in the home?

One of the first questions you need to assess is how long you think you will stay at your current residence. Or, if you leave the residence will you decide to use it as a rental property? This is an important question because there is always going to be some associated cost with a refinance. Knowing how long you think you will live in the home can help you decide, in part, what is the right type of mortgage to get when you refinance, and will also be a factor when ascertaining a breakeven analysis from doing the refinance.

2. How much is it going to cost?

Sometimes you will see the term "zero-cost financing" or "zero-cost refinance." Remember that there is always a cost to do business. Sometimes the cost will be represented in items such as closing costs or paying points to buy down your mortgage rates. Sometimes, the lender will loan you the money at a higher interest rate and choose to absorb the costs of doing the refinance. It is also possible that costs will just be rolled into the loan making your home mortgage balance slightly larger without materially affecting the interest payments.

3. How much will you save monthly?

Once you calculate all of the numbers for doing the refinance, you should be able to come up with how much money you will save monthly. Remember, all of the refinancing in the world doesn't do a lot of good if you don't put the savings to good use. This may mean paying down your consumer debt quicker, increasing your retirement contributions at work, or simply making the same mortgage payment to the lender which will pay down your mortgage quicker. Just don't spend it!

4. What is your breakeven number?

Once you know how much the refinance is going to cost you and you know how much you are going to save monthly, you can calculate how many months you need to stay in the home to break even. This is why the first question about how long you will live in the home is important. If it is going to take you three years to break even and you might move in the next year or two, the refinance may not be worth it especially if you have no plans to use it as a rental home.

5. Did you realize you just reset the clock?

The last point I'll make is that if you exchange a new 30-year mortgage for the old 30-year mortgage, you reset the 30-year clock. This seems obvious, but people who refinance 3 or 4 times over a 10-year period may be adding what would normally be a 30-year mortgage life into a 40-year mortgage life. One good part of goal planning is to try to pick an age where you want the mortgage paid off in full for good. This may be at the time you try to make working optional such as 50, 55, or 60. Not having a mortgage gives you lots of freedom for choices about what do and creates a much less stressful environment.

You should always consult a qualified mortgage broker, financial advisor, or CPA before making a major decision to go through all of the math on whether refinancing makes sense. It can be a Smart Money Move. And lastly, remember that interest rates won't stay low forever.

Should You Pay Off The Mortgage?

One of the more difficult questions that I hear from younger and older people alike is whether or not it is a good idea to pay off their mortgage. If you have locked in a low interest rate recently when they were hovering around all-time lows, you are probably happy about not having to shop for a new mortgage. If your rate is in the 3% to 4% range, you may be wondering if you should take your excess monthly discretionary income to pay down your home note faster. Or, if it be a better idea to take that cash and invest it for the long term. This decision has both financial and emotional ramifications, so let's review the pros and cons of paying off your mortgage.

The first part of this analysis is the black and white calculations on whether your money can work harder for you than the interest rate you are paying on your debt. Let's say that your mortgage rate is currently 4% on a 30-year fixed note. This is the interest rate you are borrowing the money at for the next thirty years. However, most people will get a tax deduction on the interest they pay every year when they fill out their itemized deductions, so you need to calculate your "real" cost of borrowing. It will be something less than 4%. Let's say in this scenario that the real "after-tax" cost of borrowing is going to be 3.6%. This is an important number to ascertain in the "pay off the mortgage" analysis because what you need to determine next is whether or not you can earn 3.6% on an after-tax basis on the investment where you invest your excess cash. The term "after-tax" is paramount because depending on your tax bracket, an investment that earns 5% could actually net you less money than the after-tax interest rate on the mortgage. You also need to consider whether the investment opportunity is guaranteed or what level of risk you are willing to take relative to paying the mortgage off. One final piece of consideration is liquidity of your money. When you pay down the mortgage quicker, you may lose access to your capital should an emergency or opportunity arise. This is a new factor to consider in this economy because it is harder to get equity lines of credit from the bank. The growth of the real estate is irrelevant in this analysis because the top line value of the house will grow the same whether or not you pay off the mortgage quicker.

The second part of this analysis is the gray area, which is: "Will paying off your mortgage make you feel emotionally better than you to today?" One consideration is how often you think you will move over the next five to ten years. If you see significant job or life changes happening in the next decade, I would be less inclined to advise you to pay off your mortgage because life changes usually require more cash liquidity. You may also want to consider whether or not your company will buy your house out in a move as this is being done less and less in today's environment. The most crucial discussion around paying off the mortgage is how it will make you feel. If you go to work every day just to pay off your obligations and that's why you work, I would tell you to pay down the note as quickly as you can. Having no mortgage can provide an uplifting feeling that no matter what happens in your job situation, nobody can take your home away from you. This emotional feeling gives you flexibility of life choices. Remember, some or all of your home value can also be a potential future long-term retirement asset as well. If you pay off your mortgage, then it's important to have a ready-made game plan on what you intend to do with your excess cash so it doesn't fly out the window.

Unfortunately, there is no "right" answer to this question that people ask themselves all the time. I'm a much bigger fan of paying down your debts because I think this gives you much more flexibility when it comes to job and life related decisions for your financial future. More importantly, it lightens your backpack. There are no real good studies I have seen on how much debt affects the health of Americans, but I can tell you from seeing thousands of cases, it cannot be good. As it stands today, there is nothing you'll likely find with a guaranteed rate of return to match your mortgage if you are in a 30-year fixed note. For those of you in your 40's or 50's considering these questions, ask yourself how much life and job flexibility would you have if you had no mortgage?

Should You Use A Debt Relief Program

Over the years, I have received requests from people asking for information about the various debt relief programs that advertise on television and online. Since some of these programs are scams and some are legitimate, it is important to take the appropriate steps to find the right program for you. Here are some thoughts on choosing a program that may be right for you.

1. What solutions does the company provide?

Different companies or non-profits are skilled at providing various debt relief/settlement programs. You need to consider the size of debt you are trying to negotiate down and what type of debt you are looking to reduce overall. Recognize that many of the credit card companies won't even talk with you while you are still on the proverbial stationary bicycle making minimum monthly payments. Some companies do debt consolidation, some debt negotiation/settlement, and some will deal with IRS debt as well. The more specialized the organization you choose, the better chance you have to accomplish your debt relief goal.

2. What is the cost for engagement of the debt relief company?

This can be one of the hardest parts of being able to choose a company. Some companies ask for a fee up front. These companies are the ones I like the least and are typically where you find the largest number of scams. I recommend getting involved with a debt relief company that makes its money when you get your debt negotiated and settled. Various companies will work on a fee system, a percentage commission system, or a monthly fee, which you need to be certain will end once you complete the process. You should be 100% certain that you see a contract in writing before you engage with any of these companies so what they tell you and what it is in writing are one and the same. Remember, that any percentage savings (for example, "we will save you 80% on your debt") does not include the fees that you will pay to the debt relief company. As a rule of thumb, plan that you will see a net savings of 30% to 50% when it is all said and done.

3. Is this company reliable?

Check with the Better Business Bureau to see if the debt relief company you are considering has a quality rating with no complaints. Also check the Internet to see if the company has had any items posted on a local or national complaint board. You should ask if they are part of any local organizations such as a Chambers of Commerce. However, nothing can serve you better than asking for references of three customers you can talk to who have used the debt relief company and actually saved money.

4. Is this a scam?

While scams can sometimes be hard to detect, be sure to get everything in writing and don't pay any upfront fees. Do not give any of these organizations a direct link to a credit card or bank account, and make sure if they ask for an ongoing fixed monthly fee that the contract stipulates how the agreement ends. Scammers are very skilled at making a lot of promises, and work very well at getting around contracts.

5. How will this affect your credit score?

If a company negotiates on your behalf for debt relief, you will want to make sure they also work with the debt company to give you a satisfactory rating for paying off the debt. While the debt relief may save you money, it could end up hurting your credit score if the items are reported incorrectly, which can cost you money in higher interest rates in the future.

Whatever route you go down, remember that you are the CEO of your family/personal finances. A good CEO gets several options when presented with a difficult business decision and weighs the pros and cons of the entire situation. Even if you feel like the debt could potentially make you bankrupt, you need to think about what will get your company (your personal finances) back on track to achieve your financial goals.

Chapter 3

Smart Every Day Money Moves

In this chapter, we're going to talk about basic things that you can do to help save money. We'll start by talking about your habits, particularly when it comes to food and dining out and we'll go all the way through to talking about money with your partner – hitting just about everything else in between. These tips are meant to be quick and dirty tips that can be done with just a few minor tweaks in your everyday life.

10 Ways to Cut Your Food Bill

Is your family what I call an equal opportunity grocery shopper? When you look at your debit or credit card statement, do you wonder the reasons why Kroger, Publix, Trader Joe's, and Whole Foods all show up as a line item? For individuals and families alike, the 'food' bill has become one of the largest line items in the household budget. Food can include groceries, dining out, and even meals on vacation. Here are ten smart money moves tips on how to trim the 'fat' from the food bill this year.

1. Make a list.
Purchase some sort of notepad from any store or create a list by searching for grocery list under images in Google for free.

2. Sunday night grilling.
It's hard to prepare all of the meals for the week. Consider grilling up

a bunch of chicken or steak in bulk on a Sunday night and keeping it to add to meals to bring into work during the week.

3. Avoid small bags of stuff.
Buying loose candy from the sweet shop, overpriced bags of beef jerky, or small bags of nuts can put a dent in the food budget during the year. Buying in larger packages and then parceling the contents out on your own can save you money.

4. Look for coupons.
It wouldn't really be a list if it didn't entail finding coupons. Whether this is a scanned card program with the grocery store or using a deal aggregator site, just search for coupons before dining out or bringing food into the house.

5. Eat half your meal.
I know leftovers aren't always as tasty as the original, but if only half the meal is eaten then bring the other half home and you will save money in the long run. You'll also be less likely to order more at your dining out experience.

6. Have a potpourri night.
Many people head to grocery shop before they have exhausted their own pantry. There is a reason they bought some of the items that are stocked on their shelves. Make a meal with what is already there.

7. Dine out on off nights.
The majority of BOGO deals (buy one, get one), 50% off nights, and kid's eat free nights are on Sunday, Monday, and Tuesday. Try to eat out one of these days of the weeks versus going out on a weekend when prices are prime time.

8. Start a small garden.

The organic produce aisle is pricy. You can spend big money for items such as mint and basil. But you don't have to have a green thumb to grow your own herbs. Buy a few containers for the porch or deck, have a little fun and save some money.

9. Drink water.

Not the bottled water! Just drink water from the tap (with or without a Brita filter) or from the refrigerator. Water is free – and low calorie, too.

10. Look for store brands or house specials.

Buy generic brands for vitamins or cereal and to save money on each grocery shopping experience. If eating out, find the local restaurant's special items because odds are they make more of it and the price can be less expensive than one-off items on the menu.

Do You Eat Out Too Much?

Is disposable income sneaking out the financial back door? One of the causes could be eating out every week. With a family of five, eating out at even a simple, casual fare restaurant, such as Olive Garden or Longhorn, can run $60 to $80 with basic fountain drinks. Add in a couple of appetizers and you could be reaching $100 for a family of five. In addition, lunches at the local deli or a casual fast fare type restaurant can set you back $10 a day pretty quickly during the workweek. Total up all of the lunches and dinners, and it could be dwindling those valuable disposable dollars that can help to build a college education or retirement fund. Dining out and entertainment expenses have become a blurred line in the family budgeting process because of so many new places are treating food like art. Spending more than 5 percent of your net income probably crosses the line for dining out, becoming more than it should be as a line item within a spending plan. So, how to fix this hole in your budget?

1. It's the same old... same old.

Do you ever have those nights or weekends where you go to dine out simply because you are bored as hell from the same three meals you keep eating over and over again? In these cases, you really aren't looking to spend more money, but just figure out a way to cure your overall boredom with the routine. Beat the boredom: invite a few friends or neighbors over for a barbeque or do a potluck type dinner where everyone brings a few dishes. By having a meal with others you can actually get to sample some other dishes and come up with ideas. Another alternative can be to use a social media sites like Pinterest to try some new recipes.

2. Planning, planning, planning.

Our family has adopted a family wall calendar where we all put up the different school and business events we have for the week. If grocery shopping is on the weekend and the calendar of events for the week are already known, it can be easier to meal plan. This means you might be able to buy something frozen that you really like from the grocery or specialty store. When you don't take the time to plan, it can force you into eating random meals out that add to your expense load each month.

3. Do dessert, not dinner.

If you're planning to have a family night or even a date night with your partner, it doesn't have to cost and arm and a leg. Consider taking a walk or drive to the local ice cream shop for some tasty treats or hitting the local coffee shop for dessert instead of having dinner out. Many times when out at casual fare restaurant, doubting your decision only happens after it is already too late and the dessert is already on the way to the table. Eating dessert at these places will make it even worse. One way to cut down on these expenses is making the main meal at home and then going somewhere for dessert.

4. Breakfast for dinner.

When dining out for dinner or lunch, consider breakfast as an alternative. Breakfast choices tend to be less expensive overall than lunch or dinner options and can be a great alternative. This means going for an omelet, a stack of pancakes, or yogurt with as opposed to the regular meal. It can be a fun and refreshing way to lighten things up.

Growing up as a kid, eating was truly a treat in the family. With the convenience of fast food and casual fare restaurants, it's easy to turn dining out into a four or five night a week routine. Consider closely how this can impact the overall budget and how that money plays into your overall financial goals. We all need to work on achieving the right balance between spending and saving.

Five Ways To Save Money At Department Stores

There's nothing worse than having a white-coated clinician waft some newly branded perfume in your face as you gently stroll through the front doors of the department store. Anyone can get lost in a department store. Some have three or four floors and it can take an afternoon to enjoy the ultimate in department stores: Harrod's. People shop at different department stores for different reasons, but here are five smart money moves if you are set on spending an afternoon trawling through racks of clothes or traipsing up and down escalators looking for a bargain.

1. Start at the clearance racks.

The upscale department stores are stocked full of great merchandise. Unfortunately, they don't put it in the front of the store where most people start shopping. Work your way toward the back of the store or to a particular department and get to the clearance rack before looking at anything else. Otherwise that great new fancy patterned shirt first seen at the front door will be the first purchase. This can be especially true for shoes.

2. Get to know one department store well.

All department stores have their own methodology on how they move inventory and create sales. It's difficult to mentally manage the deals between ten different department stores. For example, Nordstrom may have a dozen separate customer incentive programs. These can include special shopping days to earn more points, cash referrals for new customers, half-off yearly men's sales, anniversary sales, and even rewards for writing reviews at www.nordstrom.com. No matter what the store, consider learning the footprint of one department store to save big.

3. Only go with gift cards.

Everyone hates getting gift cards to stores that will never be used. Gift cards for a birthday, anniversary, or the holidays can save money by offering an overall budget from the start. With a $100 gift certificate, create a spending limit of another $100 to prevent a free-for-all shopaholic moment just because of some free money.

4. Become friends with a salesperson.

Everyone runs in the other direction when they notice a salesperson coming in their direction. No one wants to be smothered when browsing through a department store. Often, there is the feeling that a salesperson tries to get shoppers to purchase more and more merchandise. However, many of the salespeople know when inventory is changing or when sales and deals are coming. It might make sense to get to know one or two of them to get the inside scoop.

5. Get free samples.

There is nothing better than a few little sample goodies to try out different products. When it comes to men's or women's cologne, a small sample spritzer can last a week or two. Sometimes there are free facial scrub, shaving cream, or lip balm giveaways.

For some, going to the local or mall department store is a favorite pastime activity. These five smart money moves can make the experience a little better by potentially saving a few dollars.

5 Ways To Cut Down Your Cell Phone Bill

Many of my clients talk about how they have bills that continually increase year after year. Two of the main monthly costs that keep going up and up for many families are the cable bill and the cell phone bill. Since mobile companies offer so many different types of plans with minutes, data, texting, and other additional options, it's important to review your family's cell phone bill each year to see how keep costs to a minimum. Here are five ways to potentially cut down cell phone bills.

1. Who are your Top Ten?

Most of the mobile phone companies will offer some type of free minute program around the ten friends and family contacted the most. If a family bill has 25% to 50% of total minutes within those ten numbers, it can be lowered to the amount of minutes needed for a master plan which could help save money to the bottom line.

2. Unlimited texting (or limit the minutes).

Children who have a mobile phone tend to have a complete opposite talk to text ratio from adults. Most of the kids who are under the age of 17 will use about 80 to 90% texting and only 10% to 20% talking, whereas most parents' of teenagers will be the opposite. If texting amounts are getting up in the thousands, the best option is likely to go to an unlimited texting plan to cut the overall bill. If choosing to go with a smaller amount of texts, then it might make sense to spend $5 a month to put the cap on each child so they don't exceed the limits where most of the extra charges come from.

3. Only change your phone when an upgrade is available.
Most of the mobile phone companies, allow you to upgrade a phone without incurring the full cost of the phone every two years. It can be easy to get caught up with the latest and greatest technology and want to change phones every year, but this can really add significant cost to the bottom line of the bill. One consideration with the new iPhones or other expensive android devices is to buy insurance in case the phone breaks. The new iPhones can cost an astronomical amount of money when the phone gets cracked, so getting insurance (especially for kids) may be a smart money move.

4. See if your employer has a discount program.
Many large corporations have something called an employee mall. In the employee mall (or benefits booklet), an employer will have negotiated a master discount program with Verizon, AT&T, Sprint, or one of the other major carriers. These discount offers can range from 10% to 25% depending on the carrier. In addition, a phone plan tied into a family plan with kids can save $40 per month or more.

5. Don't dial 411.
With all of the accessibility today through data plans and access to the internet, there really should be very little reason to dial 411 anymore. For most of the cell phone companies charge a fee of $1.99 each time 411 is dialed. Do that a few times per month and it will quickly equal $10 a month of extra charges just to grab a phone number.

As smart phones and tablets become more of an integrated part of our lives and the lives of our children, it's important to do research before making any type of impulsive purchase. As the CEO of your family finances, it's vital to manage both the fixed and variable costs of the income statement. The mobile phone bill should be reviewed several times per year generally using the usage analysis offered by on the cell phone company's website. Watch the bill closely, to avoid dialing 911 vs. 411 if you get a monthly bill that shocks you!

Organizing Your Food Budget

Here is a short list of six food related money saving books which help improve the bottom line in 2015.

1. *The Coupon Mom's Guide To Cutting Your Grocery Bills In Half* by Stephanie Nelson
In the blogging world, Coupon Mom has been a top five blog for as long as I have ever been involved with the blogging scene. Stephanie can show how to save thousands of dollars on bills without sacrificing quality at all.

2. *Paleo On A Budget, Eating Healthy, Saving Money* by Elizabeth McGaw
Learn how to save money and eat like royal ancestors. She has a great recipe for oversized meatballs and a variety of dishes that can help get both physically and financially fit.

3. *We Use Coupons, You Should Too* by Nathan Engles
Since Mrs. Coupon came already, it's probably a good idea to meet the Mr. Coupon as well. This is a cheap read for only $5.00 and Mr. Engles personally got himself out of $80,000 of debt by using coupons and other strategies that can save money.

4. *Grow Your Food For Free* by Dave Hamilton
Tired of paying big prices for the organic produce at the grocery

store? According to Hamilton, recycle and reuse materials creatively and gather everything needed to grow food on a budget. This is a practical guide that can show how to save money throughout all seasons of the year.

5. *Money For Food: Your Piggy Bank: A Guide to Spending and Saving for Kids!* By Mary Elizabeth Salzmann
If you ever wanted to teach kids the concepts such as price, quantity, and quality, then this is a great read to help become better stewards of the family budget. At some point, children will have to make these decisions on their own. What better way to teach them the value of the dollar and help them make good food choices.

6. *101 Recipes For Preparing Food In Bulk* by Richard Helweg
There is a reason for the proliferation of the Costco's, BJ's, and Sam's Clubs over the past ten years. The simple truth is that a dollar doesn't stretch as far as it used to as food inflation is rising at a rate faster than normal inflation. This book provides tips about how to save big money by preparing food in bulk.

If you don't have the time to read all six of these, pick just one on your next airplane flight and see if it doesn't improve your bottom line!

Investing On A Student Budget
According to www.billshrink.com, the average student spends about $1,000 on Spring Break. By the way, less than half of that $1,000 is spent on food and lodging, so guess where the rest of the money goes during party time? Getting an investment plan started as a student can be really difficult, especially if you are making money in part time jobs or have income coming in sporadically over the summertime. However, it is very important to your financial future that you begin getting some type of investing program in place so you can

get using to saving money for your future. Here are three types of accounts you can open and add to that don't require a huge minimum investment to open an account.

1. www.computershare.com.

Through Computershare, you can invest in something called the McDirect program for McDonald's stock. In a plan like McDonalds, the minimum investment for a custodial account is $100 or $500 for a regular account. Today, you only need to buy one share of stock within a custodial account to open up a Computershare plan. When McDonalds pays dividends, they will automatically buy fractional shares of the stock and reinvest those dividends. In addition, you can add money anytime to you like for a nominal fee to purchase additional full or fractional shares of stock.

2. www.oneshare.com.

This is a great website to purchase presents for family members or friends when they had a new baby. Oneshare is the ultimate way to connect someone to their favorite company. You can choose from hundreds of different companies to literally buy your child one share of their favorite company, whether it is Krispy Kreme or Disney. The stock that you buy can be matted and framed to hang in your dorm room or simply sent in the mail to you. After you purchase the initial one share of stock, you can add money along the way to continue to buy fractional shares while the dividends automatically get reinvested. There is an upfront registration fee for about $50, but after that initial fee you'll be on your way to stock ownership.

3. Discount Brokerage House.

At most of the discount brokerage houses such as TD Ameritrade, E*Trade, Schwab, Fidelity, and Vanguard, you can open an account to invest in low cost indexed exchange traded funds. By setting up some type of ACH with your bank account, you can add money to these accounts on a regular basis.

With many students having tons of student debt coming out of college, any head start that a college graduate can give themselves can help ease the transition into real life. While most kids may not make a ton of money during college, starting an investment program may be just the class you need to become a straight A student.

How to Budget Your Next Vacation

A client retired a few years ago and is in the midst of publishing his own travel book; an individual with a true knack for knowing how to budget out a vacation. One of the principles he's stuck to over a lifetime while becoming wealthy is to not take a vacation that he did not already pay for in advance of the trip (including spending money). He may book a vacation to go to Italy one year from now, and if the trip will cost $4,000 he will actually make payments of $333 a month over the next 12 months. By the time the vacation is upon him, he can really enjoy the excursion to a far away destination because he won't have the debt lingering over his head when he comes back to the United States. While we all may not be able to take this exact methodology, discussing some of the key points on how to budget your vacations into your overall household income might get us a few steps closer.

1. Vacations should be a 2% to 3% line item within a normal household budget.

One of the very challenging issues to tackle as the CEO of your family finances is how much of a percentage should vacation and travel constitute of your overall expense load as a family. If you make $200,000 per calendar year, your overall yearly vacation spend shouldn't be more than $4,000 to $6,000 overall. Part of the issue why many households fall behind each year is due to the overspending on categories like meals/entertainment and travel/vacations. The first key is to set the actual budget within this expense category, which allows you to work backwards on how many trips you can afford and where you will take them. Anything above a 5% spend in this one category is extremely dangerous.

2. Decide what you want to get out of the vacation.

This statement is all about setting expectations. We get to see the lifestyles of the rich and famous on regular and reality TV shows alike today all the time. Start considering the following: what is the purpose of my vacation? Am I making memories for me as a parent as I spend time with my kids? What kinds of activities am I interested in doing on the vacation? Is there a part of the United States or the rest of the world that I always wanted to see? Is this about getting family together overall? What exactly is your raison d'être for making this spend? Otherwise, if you are a people pleaser you might pick the fanciest hotel in the nicest of destinations only to see you and your kids having the most miserable time. I want to underscore that if you are taking little kids away, they aren't likely to remember many of your trips years down the road, so don't fall for the trap that a Magic Kingdom memory is going to be something your kids cherish for the rest of their lives. The part they remember the most is the pool at the hotel and the grilled cheese at the local restaurant.

3. What kind of points do you have available?

Destination getaways are well aware of the prime seasons to hike prices such as summer, Christmas, spring break, etc. Check into the blackout periods for your airline and hotel point programs to make sure you can actually use them for your trip. In addition, at certain junctures in the calendar year you can stretch out your points or get a round trip ticket for a lower number of points. It's important to maximize these point programs because it may leave you with only paying some basic taxes or ticketing fees.

4. Plan your spending money.
It's vacation, so as you begin to unwind and relax so will your wallet. What the heck honey, we're on vacation!!! The moral of the story is to not let the plastic run the financial limits it can carry. Plan in advance how much spending cash you will bring for extracurricular activities, tourist attractions, meals, and souvenirs. Otherwise, what do you think you'll be inclined to do once you get there to get the kids to stop screaming for just five minutes? You will end up opening up your wallet and turning yourself upside down.

Having planned out thousands of family finances over the past two decades, vacation spending is a constant black hole you will have to deal with every year. Since it is the early spring of 2014, take a step back now to plan out Spring Break, the summer, and holiday season to determine just what spending limit to set for family vacations. Otherwise what you will end up with is a handful of photos, a few vacation trinkets, and a nasty credit card hangover.

Doing A Wedding On A Budget
Will you marry me? That magical phrase is shared between two people in love every day whether it happens on a baseball score-board or with the entire family watching in the living room. Last Year student debt for Generation Y graduates approached an all-time high. According to a recent *USA Today* article, about two-thirds of college grads in the Class of 2013 graduated with some student loan debt. The average debt was about $28,000. The real question couples should be asking when they tie the knot is "Am I marrying you or your debt?" It's important to have these discussions as financial items including credit score; it can have an impact on loan status and

job employment as the two futures grow together. Here are five smart money moves tips to consider for wedding planning so as to have fun and within a reasonable budget.

1. The day of the week.

Saturdays are generally the most common day of the week to get married. If the weekend is the only choice, Sunday can be a better day of the week to negotiate a deal especially if considering doing it at night. Many venues will be able to offer the same sit down dinner on a Sunday night versus a Saturday night at a better price. Obviously doing a wedding of any proportion on a weekday is extremely difficult, but will be the least expensive route if swinging the planning. Remember, the day of the week may also dictate flight and hotel prices for guests as well.

2. The venue.

If running tight on the overall budget, it might be a good idea to use the backyard of a parent's home or that of a close friend to entertain guests if possible. There may be other low cost venues, but this type of outdoor wedding with (or without) a tent can save thousands of dollars. With this type of wedding, money saved can be spent on decorations, food, and fun.

3. The food.

Avoiding a sit down dinner and opting for a buffet will generally save money right off the top. If doing a more causal wedding, then doing a limited choice buffet such as beef or chicken barbeque with some sides can be a relatively inexpensive idea. Also limiting the bar to wine, beer, and perhaps one or two house drinks along with iced tea and lemonade can still pull off a good time. Remember, the more fancy the venue and the more courses served the higher the budget will run.

4. The music.

There can be a five piece band with two singers or even a top notch local DJ, but the truth is that it's a smaller wedding in a local or backyard venue, then the music choice can be anything. Create a music list and spend a few bucks on the right outdoor wireless equipment and can get a microphone to still do toasts and announcements throughout the wedding.

5. The photography and video.

With many young budding photographers and videographers starting their own small businesses, there are usually good deals to shoot the wedding professionally. There are many recent college graduates from colleges that specialize in this field and the new breed of photographer can get their business up and going quickly after graduation. To really lower cost, approach one of the local schools (like SCAD in Atlanta) to find someone to shoot the wedding at low or no cost. The cheapest option may be to give each guest a disposable camera or leave one on the table to take pictures. There are apps where guests can use their smart phones to take pictures and then they go to a website that allows to personally obtaining photos.

Your wedding day will go by in the blink of an eye, but its memories will last a lifetime. The last thing to do is make a bad financial move and end up in more debt.

Discussing Money As A Married Couple

When you get married and take your vows, it goes something like this: I take you to be my lawful wife/husband/partner, to have and to hold, for better, for worse, for richer, for poorer, in sickness and in health, until death do us part. It does say for richer or poorer, but unfortunately many couples across America just don't spend time discussing money. More often than not today, there are separate accounts, unmerged finances, and she pays this and he pays that. The more secretive and separate things are in a financial relationship, the worse it always turns out to be whether it be in a household or in a business partnership.

1. Set financial ground rules.
It's true that each partner needs to have some independence, so it is very easy to set up some individual checking accounts (or expense accounts) so each person has some freedom to do some of the small things they want to do on a month-to-month basis. However, before merging accounts together and getting married, set the guidelines of how to handle money from a household perspective.

2. Always consider the family's finances first.
Money is such an integral part of our lives, that good, bad, or in-different not having these conversations can lead to a ton of stress especially in a spender/saver relationship. Avoid becoming resentful every time a new purchase is made, but rather feel good about the direction of the finances in the family.

3. Discuss joint savings goals.
First and foremost, take time to discuss how much to save to reach joint goals. There will be much less friction when savings is taken care of up front. Agree on who is going to pay the bills. One person takes charge of paying the monthly bills. Decide how to communicate about money. Lastly, make sure there is a way to easily access al joint accounts (with the exception of those little individual checking accounts) so there doesn't seem to be anything sneaky going on with the money.

4. Share your money biography.
Everyone has a different childhood, money experiences, and attitudes

about money and what it means will always be different from person to person. When you take those vows, you would obviously love it the richer comment becomes the outcome versus the poorer. The couples that discuss and share their finances have a much better chance of financial independence than those that don't discuss the subject at all.

Discussing money is undoubtedly a touchy subject. But discussing your financial past and present with your partner can lead to a happier financial future.

Four Money Moves To Make When You Turn 40

Generation X is classically defined at people born between the years 1965 and 1979. This means within the next few years, all Gen X'ers will be 40 or older. If life begins at 40, then it must be certain that making smart money moves should fold into that new beginning. Whether you are woefully drowning in student debt, just getting married, or starting to make some serious money, here are four smart money moves to consider when you turn the age of 40.

1. Admit your Mistakes... they are natural.

The kind of mistakes we are discussing fall into three categories: financial, personal and professional. It's OK that you've made some mistakes (we all have) but now we have to start correcting them.

- *Financial Mistakes - If you have spending money like a drunken sailor, making sure you are seeing all the best concerts and dining at the fanciest restaurants, don't beat yourself up. If you have piled up debt or lost money on a private investment deal, there is still time. Just be make sure you recognize the mistake(s) so you don't continue to make them.*

- *Personal Mistakes - Sure, you may have had a costly divorce or loaned money to someone in a relationship that turned sour. Even if you are paying child support, you can still build a plan for the next 20 years that will help ensure your own success.*
- *Professional Mistakes - Perhaps you held on to a job too long or missed an opportunity for a promotion. Generating revenue will be one of the major keys to the next 20 years of your financial life. No matter what stage you are at, now is a great time to assess how you will grow your own top line revenue.*

2. Run the retirement numbers.

You aren't a kid anymore… I've seen all kinds of articles that now say normal retirement age may be at 70 or later because we are living longer. I say that the average Gen X'er is half way burned out already and wondering how they can work, but focus on the projects they want to do versus the ones that they have to do. It's that notion if money were no object, what would you be doing with your life? My best professional guess is that more than half of you reading this would change jobs tomorrow if it weren't for the money. This means you really need to figure out where you need to be financially to make that happen.

3. Revisit your life insurance.

Whatever you think you need, boost it. The majority of 40 year-olds underestimate how much life insurance they need. Do you really think your family could make it on 1 million dollars for the rest of their life? When considering health insurance, do it now! You are still at the age where most of you can get better rates on life insurance. Just like a car, we all get wear and tear on our bodies. Make sure you get as much life insurance as you can while the going is still good. If you opt for term life insurance, make sure your policy is convertible. You don't know what your health will be like at the age of 60 or 70.

4. Choose wisely.

At 40, you will start to have choices to make that can greatly impact your financial future. If you choose to do a 30-year refinance, realize that the mortgage might not be paid off until you are 70. If you are saving for your kids' college education, make sure you don't over save for them and under save for your retirement. Most importantly, make sure you don't pile up debt. Debt will not only drag you down financially, but it can cripple you emotionally.

If life begins at 40, begin life the right way with these four smart financial moves and put yourself in a position to make work optional one day.

Chapter 4

Investing for Long-Term Success

Now that we have discussed the personal finance basics, it's time to start thinking about investing. An important element in securing your financial future is to invest your money wisely. In this chapter, we'll talk about the basics (and not so basics) of investing, including: building cash reserves *before* you start investing, risk tolerance, asset allocation, mutual funds, IRAs, and finally, how to get the next generation interested in investing.

How much should you keep in cash reserves?

Building a solid financial plan is similar to building a strong house. If you create a secure foundation and structure for the house, it is likely to stand up against all of the elements over the course of the years to come. Many financial plans fail because they are not built on solid foundations. The two biggest mistakes people make when developing a financial plan are that they forget to build up an appropriate cash reserve and/or have adequate risk management protection put into place before beginning to invest. There are often various numbers thrown around in the media about what is an adequate cash reserve to have in your financial plan, but here are some thoughts for consideration on how much money to have in checking, savings, and other short-term investment instruments.

The first question you should be asking is whether you are employed (and whether there is stability at your job) or whether you are self-employed. My opinion is that people who own a business should have about double the normal cash reserve of someone who is gainfully employed with a corporation. The second question is whether or not you anticipate any major life changes over the next year. This could include the birth of child, an upcoming marriage/divorce, or potentially changing jobs or moving to another part of the country. These changes often create the need for more cash as your cash flow will likely be unstable. The third question is what major changes do you see happening with your employer over the next 12 to 24 months. Do you see more layoffs coming or a department restructure? Do you see the company cutting the commission/bonus plans for salespeople? Questions like these are important for impacting cash reserve. Lastly, do you plan to retire over the next year or two? This can impact how much you have to beef up your cash reserves. With all that said, here are my thoughts on what you need to consider having in savings for emergencies or opportunities that may arise.

1. Gainfully employed by a corporation.

If you (and/or your partner/spouse) are employed by a Fortune 500 company, you will most likely need about six months of monthly expenses squirreled away in a cash reserve account. If you work for a smaller corporation or are worried about job stability, then I recommend having nine to twelve months in savings. In my mind, the old rule of thumb of three months is too little given the economic uncertainty we face today and how quickly people change employers.

2. Self-employed.

If you run a business that is less than five years old, I suggest that you build up at least a year's income equivalent in cash reserves. This could be some combination between business checking cash and personal savings cash. Until your business maintains a level of consistency of monthly cash flow, you should maintain a larger bank account in case the business encounters a rough patch. For business owners, it is more important to create a business plan that accounts for expansion and whether cash, cash flow, loans, and/or equity will capitalize future growth.

3. Retired.

For folks entering their first year of retirement, I recommend at least twelve to eighteen months of cash. Typically, the jubilation phase of retirement (first couple of years) is where retirees overspend against a normal budget until they get into a regular groove of what they will be doing in the next phase of their lives. About 24 months into retirement, you can get a better gauge on overall expenses and then set the bar for a more normal cash reserve.

I recognize that it can be frustrating to have lots of money in cash because interest rates are nonexistent on checking account and are less than paltry on savings and money market accounts. Even Certificates Of Deposit (CDs) do not offer the kind of rates they did in the 90s or early 2000s. However, cash reserves within a financial plan provide set-aside resources to take care of unforeseen expenses that will arise in your financial situations. Or, if there is a unique opportunity, cash reserves can be used to take advantage of that opportunity without destroying the integrity of retirement savings, college education savings, and/or other financial goals. Follow these rules of thumb and you'll build a slab of financial concrete that can weather even the worst of storms.

Don't Bet It All On Black

Many years ago, Wesley Snipes was in a movie called Passenger 57. It was basically a film about a one man's attempt to take on an airliner hijacking. During the course of the movie, he gets engaged in the time-honored bad action hero scene where he talks smack to the European terrorists over the phone. During the phone call Wesley Snipes says, "You ever play roulette?" The mad European terrorist replies, "On occasion." Snipes responds with the famous phrase, "Well, let me give you a piece of advice. Always bet on black!" In the world of money and investing, we have been taught time and time again that is it important to build a diversified portfolio to manage the risk that different investment classes can have in our portfolio. However, time and again people come to me for financial advice who have previously gone with a "Bet It All On Black" investment strategy by putting most of their eggs in one stock, one asset class, or one business venture. Here are three smart money move ideas on how to prevent from losing the game of roulette by betting it all on black.

1. Set up an Investment Policy Statement.

An Investment Policy Statement (IPS) is a document, generally between an investor and her or his investment manager, recording the agreements the two parties have with regard to how the investor's money is to be managed. The presence of an IPS helps to clearly communicate to all relevant parties the procedures, investment philosophy, guidelines and constraints to be adhered to by all parties. It can be viewed as a directive from the client to the investment manager about how the money is to be managed, but at the same time the IPS also provides the guidelines for all investment decisions and responsibilities of each party. The key to the Investment Policy Statement is to limit how much of one position you put your cash into at any given time. For example, an IPS might state that the portfolio cannot hold more than 10% in one individual fund or stock.

2. Have an exit strategy.

Whether you made money on a particular investment because of skill or luck, the problem is not having a predetermined game plan on how you will exit that investment whether it is an individual stock, a piece of real estate, or a business venture. Far too often over the years, we have seen people get carried away with the thought that the investment they own just simply could not lose money. This type of dangerous "Bet it All on Black" thinking can be very dangerous to building long term wealth.

3. Get all of the information.
Have you ever heard of someone who invested money in a business that was sure to triple in value? Or perhaps you know a person that bought a "sure-to-make-a-return" condominium off of some remote beach in the United States? Maybe it was a stock tip for a technology company that was supposed to quadruple in the next year? Before you make any type of investment, be sure that you have reviewed all of the information carefully. Read the prospectus, examine the profit and loss statements, and spend time doing your due diligence.

Building wealth is a very difficult mountain to climb. Almost every investor at some point in their life spots an opportunity that they believe will get them to the peak more quickly. It's important to make sure you never bet all your money on black, red, or a specific number – no matter how sure you are that the investment is sure to make millions. If you make the wrong decision, you'll be sure be sitting in the back of the plane forever.

How Risky Are You?
Have you ever really tried to determine what your real risk tolerance is when it comes to investing? By nature, most people will tell you that they are not afraid of risk. They will tell you that they don't mind that things will go up and down in value. That is, of course, until those investments actually start going down. It's only when the monthly statements are down, your real estate is down, or some private equity deal is going down the tank that you can really determine

your threshold for risk. Because risk is a normal part of investing, maybe it's time to determine just how risky you are.

The amount of risk you take with your investments should be directly proportional to how much time you have to let the investments work for you. I have always used the analogy of a swimming pool to discuss risk with clients. Most community or neighborhood swimming pools have a baby pool and a main pool swimming area. The baby pool is typically only six inches to a foot deep. The main swimming pool usually starts out with an area that is one to three feet deep, moves to the middle part that slopes down from four to seven feet deep, and then the deep end, which is typically 7 to 10 feet deep. If each foot represented one year of time that your money was to be invested, you could translate how many years you need to stay in a particular investment to warrant the risk you will take with the investment.

Here's how it works. If you have six months to one year to reach a financial goal, you really can't take on much risk and probably belong in the baby pool. These may be investments like savings accounts, money market accounts, or short term CDs. If you have one to three years to a financial objective, you can take a little bit more risk and use investing instruments like longer term CDs and short-term bonds. As you move deeper into the pool, if your goal is four to seven years away, this may be the first time you can consider intermediate type bonds or the stock market if you have more than five years. Lastly, if you have seven to ten years to a goal you can begin to look at more aggressive investments such as emerging markets, technology, or longer-term real estate investments. The big mistake most people make is to choose investments that are not suitable for their time horizon before needing to reach a financial goal. This is why people who invest in the stock market for a goal only a year away can be taking on abnormally high and undue risk.

There are all sorts of tools that can be found online or through a financial professional that can help you determine your overall risk tolerance. The last ten years have been marked by major ups and downs within investment portfolios, so it may be time to revisit the risk you take for your financial future!

The Three I's of Investing and Risk

With Moody's Investment Service downgrading more than a dozen global banks to reflect declining profitability, and the Euro Zone looking to be in grave financial crisis, many investors are asking how to find investments that carry no risk. Some of these investors are folks that are retired and looking for current income while others are at the twenty yard line approaching the end zone of their retirement day. So where do you find an investment that carries no risk?

Unfortunately, every single type of investment carries some inherent risk. Learning how to balance risk, being timely with your investments and knowing what risks to take at what time can ultimately determine the success or failure of your overall investment plan. When it comes to today's main risks facing investors, here are the three big I's with respect to investing and risk.

1. Inflation risk.

Inflation risk, sometimes known as purchasing power risk is the chance that the cash flows from an investment won't be worth as much in the future because of changes in purchasing power due to rising inflation. Since the United States Federal Reserve recently added tremendous liquidity to the US Commercial Banking system, many people worry that the quick rise in money supply will inevitably affect a rise in inflation. So, with all of the fears going on around the world, one would think that potentially leaving money in the bank would be risk-free. If your bank account is earning 1% guaranteed and FDIC insured you will see your account statement go up. However, you need to consider that if inflation is 4% or 5%, you are effectively losing the purchasing power of your money. This is a good example on how a risk-free investment could actually carry risk.

2. Interest rate risk.

Interest rate risk is essentially the risk that a bond's (security) value will change due to a change in interest rates. Interest rates and bonds generally have a see saw or inverse type relationship. That means a bond's value can actually go down when interest rates rise and a bonds value can actually go up when interest rates go down. The longer the maturity of the bond, the more of a swing the bonds value can have when interest rates spike or decline. Think about it like this: if there were two kids on a see saw that weighed exactly the same amount. All of a sudden one of the kids was replaced with a much heavier kid causing the see saw to be out of balance. This is what it looks like when there is an interest rate change. While a bond may be making a consistent interest/coupon payment to you every quarter or every six months, you should keep an eye on the length of maturity of your bonds in case interest rates spike again as your bond could lose significant value – especially if you don't plan to hold the bond until it matures. If you own a bond mutual fund or bond exchange traded fund, you need to understand what the bond fund's maturity is or as more commonly known the average maturity of the bond portfolio. Although bonds can seem safe, interest rate risk could greatly affect them.

3. Investment risk.

This can mean different things to different people, but I generally think about this risk with equity investments like stocks. Typically, this includes things like business risk, valuation risk, and force of sale risk. The risk with which most people are familiar is company or business risk. We've all seen a business/franchise/company that we thought was really fantastic when it first hit the market. Our enthusiasm got us to invest dollars into that company or business, but the business model couldn't financially sustain itself. Or perhaps a new and more competitive product debuted that improved upon the product of the company you invested in at that time. It's best to diversify your assets within this investment category, but far too often investors essentially buy the same investment just at different places. It's like the bank investor who thinks buying five CDs at five different banks is a strategy for diversification.

Every investor would like the ideal situation of high growth without any risk. No matter what path you go down, you will inevitably face some type of risk within your portfolio. Having a quality financial plan to determine the overall rate of return your money needs on an after-tax basis to achieve your goals is a great starting point. Figuring out how much money you need to save to reach your goals will be an important second step. Between these two factors, you can determine what kinds of risk you want to take between your current capital base and future savings. Although there is nowhere to hide your portfolio completely from risk there is certainly a difference between riding the kiddie coaster and lightning loops. Make sure you balance your ride so you can complete it without falling out of your seat!

S.I.G.N Your Assets for a Brighter Financial Future

Asset allocation is all about the notion that different assets classes offer returns that are not perfectly correlated. As such, diversification reduces the overall risk in terms of the variability of returns for a given level of expected return. Today's world of asset allocation uses fancy pie charts that demonstrate cash, corporate bonds, international bonds, government bonds, large cap stock, mid cap stock, small cap stock, international stock, emerging markets, commodities, real estate, and many more different types of asset classes. The idea is that all of these assets classes are supposed to act and look a lot like magnets. By having a balance of these asset classes, while some areas have worse years other categories will have better years, ultimately minimizing the overall risk in the portfolio.

Even though we have the most college-educated adults in the history of the United States, very few people get a real course on personal finance. Thus, even the smartest of these people could hardly tell you much about asset allocation at all. Could one out of ten people clearly define - by actual numbers - what a large cap stock is in terms of market capitalization? Could a basic investor tell you five different emerging markets? Heck, many of them can't even clearly articulate how a bond instrument actually works. I'm going to fill you in on my smart money moves philosophy when it comes to an easy way to think about how to bucket your asset management by using the S.I.G.N. philosophy.

S- Security.

The first area of your asset allocation is determined by how much money you need to keep in the security bucket. In the good old days, the secure bucket was largely determined by what the corporation would provide you for a pension when you retired. As many of us realize today, companies hardly offer that type of benefit anymore. Consequently, we need to figure out how much of our personal S.I.G.N. needs to be guaranteed, fixed, and secure. These are the type of assets where you attempt to take our things like market risk and interest rate risk. It is possible to create your personal pension plan.

I- Income.

The second area of your asset allocation is going to be determined by how much money you need to keep in the income bucket. There are various types of income producing assets, some fixed and some variable. In the fixed income arena, we are talking about municipal bonds, U.S. Government bonds, Corporate Bonds, CDs, Treasury Inflation Protected Securities, and savings bonds. This isn't an end all and be all list, but what you are attempting to get at is what type of overall interest rate do you expect to get in return for loaning out your money. This bucket should be left largely for loanership type dollars instead of ownership type dollars. While there are equity investments such as dividend paying stocks and real estate, this new type of thought process reserves this bucket for fixed income type investing. We would normally expect some level of income to come from social security, but as many Gen X and Gen Y investors know social security may not be there for us.

G- Growth.

The third area of your asset allocation is going to be determined by how much money you need to keep in the growth bucket. The growth bucket is designed for ownership type dollars. Specifically, having money in assets such as stocks, precious metals, real estate, and other categories where you are putting dollars at risk for the potential for larger future growth. Growth investing can happen in all types of accounts including 401(k)s, IRAs, Roth IRAs, and brokerage accounts. Depending on your personal S.I.G.N., growth investing may be a larger or smaller part of the equation.

N- Need.

The final piece to the S.I.G.N. philosophy is to determine your overall need to get to your goals. This is true whether we are talking about buying a first home, planning for children's college education, or thinking longer term about your exit plan to make work optional. You have to calculate how much you will need to determine the right balance of Security, Income, and Growth as you figure out how to reach your goals (Needs).

When Is the "Right" Time to Get Back into the Market?

Many people ask "when is the right time to put money back in the stock market?" While we never know when will be the exact "right time," there have been some strategies than can help reduce your over- all risk if you are thinking about putting money back in the market.

Two of the tried and true methods that we have all known over our careers are buy and hold, which is a famous Warren Buffet strategy. The other is the notion of dollar cost averaging, which is more popu- lar, or something called dollar share averaging. Dollar cost averaging is nothing more than putting away the same dollar amount every month irrespective of what's happening in the market. As an exam- ple, in today's market, if you had a stock that was trading at $7.50 and you put away $600, and that stock went up and down over the next six months but ended at $7.50 per share you would have exactly what you had when you started six months ago.

Let's say you decided, as opposed to investing the $600 lump sum, that you would invest $100 per month in the stock/mutual fund investment irrespective if the market went up or down. The stock be- gins with the same starting price of $7.50 per share. In the first month you invest $100, the stock is at $10 per share, which allows you to buy ren shares. In the second month it goes down to $5 per share, which allows you to buy twenty shares. In month three, the stock goes back up to $10 per share, buying you ten additional shares. In month four, the stock goes back down to $5 per share, buying twenty more shares. In month five, the stock goes back up to $10 per sharing buying you ten more shares. In month six, the stock drops back down to $5 per share, buying you twenty shares. In the next month, the stock goes back to its original price of $7.50 per share. Over the six months you acquired nintey shares and today's price is $7.50.

Now this strategy doesn't always work exactly like this, but over time it can smooth out the volatility in the market. One other strategy to think about is something called dollar share averaging. As opposed to dollar cost averaging, you just buy the same amount of shares every month in a particular stock or mutual fund no matter what happens in the market. Right now, rather than dumping a lump sum of money into any one position, buy the same amount of shares every month or put the same amount of dollars away every month. This may not change how bumpy the stock market is day to day, but can perhaps reduce some of the overall risk in your investment strategy.

It's important to remember that periodic investment plans do not assure a profit and do not protect against investment loss in declining markets. Dollar-cost averaging involves continuous investment in securities regardless of fluctuating price levels of such securities, so you should deeply consider your financial ability to continue purchasing through periods of low price levels.

The ABCs of Mutual Funds

Learning the basics of how mutual funds work can be very difficult to understand. Understanding the cost to investing in these instruments can be even more difficult. By using the simple notion of the ABCs when it comes to cost structure, you can attain a basic understanding of how your costs will generally work within a mutual fund. Although in today's mutual fund environment, there are many different cost structure strategies, most investors will primarily see three in the market place.

The first type of cost structure is referred to as an **"A" Share**, or what is sometimes known as a front-end loaded mutual fund. When you invest in this type of investment structure with mutual funds, you are typically paying your financial advisor/agent/broker a fee on top of your investment. Based upon the size of your investment, the fee generally ranges from 3% to 5.75% of the initial investment. The remainder will go to work for you in the mutual fund.

The second type of cost structure is known in the industry as a **"B" Share**, or what people may describe as a back-end loaded mutual fund. When you choose to place your assets into this type of mutual fund investment, you will have no up front cost to invest your money. However, if you redeem your investment before a certain period of time, you will be subject to some level of surrender charge on your mutual fund. Typically, the redemption charges will last 5 to 6 years with a declining surrender charge scale. While the penalty varies by mutual fund company, it is typically stiffer in your first two years for an early redemption.

The third type of cost structure is referred to as a **"C" Share**, or what most investors know as a no-load mutual fund. If you think about investing in this particular type of fee structure, then you will have no fee up front when you invest your money. Most "C" Shares will charge you a small early redemption fee if you pull your money in the first year which is typically around 1%. After that, there is no fee to pull your money out at any time. Some mutual fund companies have pure no-load fund where you can come and go as you please with no mutual fund fee from the fund company. However, you will want to review if you have transaction or brokerage fees to make trades to sell your investments.

The final thing to know about the ABCs of mutual funds is to review the internal expenses, which don't reflect charges as for buying or selling mutual funds. These charges are items such as management fees, operating expenses, 12b-1 fees, and transaction costs. Typically these charges come out of your return, not out of your statement so they are often invisible to the consumer. Transaction costs are the most invisible, and the other costs can generally be reviewed at places such as morningstar.com. Transaction costs can be reviewed at personalfund.com. What is often the case is that "B" share and "C" share mutual funds have higher internal costs (invisible one) than an "A" share, which is why you hear the term "there is no free lunch to investing".

If you stick to remembering the ABCs of mutual funds, you can look at your investment statements and better understand what you bought and how much you're being charged to invest. Otherwise, you might just end up eating a bowl of alphabet soup.

Five Myths about IRA Investing

Many people in the United States are missing out on one of the best retirement opportunities – opening an IRA account. Here are five myths that I want to clear up so you can better understand how these powerful retirement vehicles can work for you.

Myth #1

You can only invest an IRA where you opened the account. I have often heard people who make a comment such as, "I have a Bank IRA." Many investors believe that they can only invest their IRA at the bank, or better yet only invest their IRA at the financial institution where they opened the account. IRAs can be invested in almost any type of investment including CDs, stocks, bonds, mutual funds, real estate, and much more. Generally you cannot invest in collectibles or life insurance with an IRA. Once you have invested your IRA, you can transfer your IRA account to another financial institution through a direct transfer or a rollover.

Myth #2

You can't contribute to a 401(k) and an IRA in the same year. According to Fidelity Investments, 52% of Americans who do not have an IRA believe that they cannot contribute to both an IRA and workplace retirement savings account in the same year. The IRA contributions may or may not be tax deductible based upon your individual situation, but all of the IRA contributions will grow on a tax-deferred basis – no matter what level of income you earn.

Myth #3

Small business owners can't open an IRA. Most small business owners are unaware of the multitude of retirement plans available for them. There are two main types of IRA plans specifically designed for business owners called a SEP-IRA plan or a SIMPLE-IRA plan. Each of these plans has different nuances depending on the income in the business, the number of employees, and the objectives of the employer. The SEP-IRA could potentially allow a small business owner to put as much as $52,000 in retirement plan contributions in 2015 for those under 50. Catch up provisions still apply to put away more money if you are over 50. Consult your financial advisor or tax specialist before making this decision.

Myth #4

Only people who are older can put money into IRA accounts. Since IRAs are tax-deferred accounts, the people who can benefit the most are the individuals who start saving the earliest. This is true because of the time value of money and the principal of compounding interest. The earlier you save, the harder the compounding of money will work for you over the long term. Even if you can only contribute $500 or $1,000 into your IRA each year, you can still fund an IRA.

Myth #5

You are unable to access your money until the age of 59 ½ without paying a penalty. Most people believe that once money is invested in an IRA, if you withdraw the funds before the age of 59 ½ that there will be a 10% penalty imposed by the IRS. However, there is a concept called taking Substantial Equal Periodic Payments (Regulation 72t), which if followed correctly, will allow you to take a minimum level of distribution without penalty before the age of 59 ½. You should consult a tax professional before deploying this strategy.

Should You Buy A DRIP Plan?

It is important for children to learn about stock investing from an early age. We all know how grandparents try to get back at us by overloading our kids with holidays full of latest gadgets and electronics that money can buy. Whether you have $20 or $200 stashed away in your kid's drawer, there is an opportunity to get your children started in the stock market. The way you can get them started is by enrolling in a dividend reinvestment plan. A dividend reinvestment program or dividend reinvestment plan (DRIP) is an equity investment option offered directly from the underlying company. The investor does not receive quarterly dividends directly as cash; instead, the investor's dividends are directly reinvested in the underlying equity. The investor must still pay tax annually on his or her dividend income, whether it is received or reinvested. Here are a few smart money move ideas to help get you started in a DRIP plan that can help secure you're child/children's financial future.

1. ComputerShare.

This is the first place I suggest going when deciding to get a kid into stock investing. When they are learning about topics like percentages in school, being able to track a stock that they would enjoy following is a great idea to buy for them. For example, through Computer-Share, my children and I were able to invest in something called the McDirect program for McDonald's stock. In a plan like McDonalds, the minimum investment for a custodial account is $100 or $500 for a regular account. Today, you only need to buy one share of stock within a custodial account to open up a ComputerShare plan. When McDonalds pays dividends, they will automatically buy fractional shares of the stock and reinvest those dividends. In addition, you can add money anytime you like for a nominal fee to purchase additional full or fractional shares of stock.

2. OneShare.

I found this website many years ago and have used it generally to purchase presents for family members or friends when they have a new baby. OneShare is the ultimate way to connect someone to their favorite company. You can choose from hundreds of different companies to literally buy your child – or a friend's child - one share of their favorite company whether it is Krispy Kreme or Disney. The stock that you buy can be matted and framed for the child, or simply sent in the mail. After you purchase the initial one share of stock, you can add money along the way to continue to buy fractional shares while the dividends automatically get reinvested. There is an upfront registration fee of about $50, but after that initial fee you'll be well on your way to stock ownership.

3. Betterinvesting.org.

The National Association of Investors Corporation is a non-profit organization that teaches individuals and investment clubs how to employ fundamental analysis to become successful long-term investors. You can get started with them for a small registration fee and then begin buying stock through a dividend reinvestment plan.

One of the great things about getting a stock plan started for your kids is that you can always go directly to the website of the company and purchase the stock. You may want to consider getting your kids involved and talk to them about the brands of companies that they truly love. This is a great place to get started, and then see if that particular company offers a DRIP program. Wouldn't it be great if your kids wanted to save more than they wanted to spend? It could be time to start dripping them toward a path to real financial success.

Chapter 5

What Uncle Sam Doesn't Want You to Know

There are few things in life as certain as death and taxes. We'll talk about death (or at least estate planning) in Chapter 9, but for now we're going to talk about taxes. More specifically, we're going to talk about how to properly plan for taxes, legally take advantage of tax deductions, and, if you are a business owner, how to structure your business and expenses related to the business in order to maximize tax efficiency. In this chapter, you'll get a sense of how to effectively estimate your tax obligations so you're not giving Uncle Sam an interest-free loan or cutting him a big check on April 15th.

Personal Finance 101 - Tax Planning Starts In The New Year

Every year I see the same thing happen when income tax time comes around. People start scurrying like little mice looking for all of their documents, getting them to their tax professional, and beginning the small holy prayer that their accountant can get them a refund. It's like some bad game of Dungeons and Dragons, and with a roll of the twenty-sided dice you win the game if your lucky number comes up on April 15th. After April 15th, you are close to a third of the way done with the year, and then can put away your documents until the dreaded tax season hits a year from now. Right?

Wrong. The number one personal finance mistake people make is focusing on preparation of income taxes in the first quarter of the year when they should be diligently planning and implementing strategies to reduce their overall tax liability for that calendar year. Since most CPAs are focused on tax preparation during tax busy season, they generally have little time to help you with tax planning for the year. Instead, they are focused on putting together neat little binders with lots of forms, knowing that if you get a refund you'll think they did a great job for the prior calendar tax year. Since tax planning begins with the end in mind, here are some key things you'll want to be doing now to manage your taxes for next year.

1. Review your withholdings or estimated taxes

Remember that your tax bill is a function of your filing status and ultimately your overall net taxable income. Whether you owe or get a refund is truly a function of whether you withheld too much money during the calendar year or too little money during the calendar year. I am constantly amazed that hardly anybody reviews these withholdings (or estimated taxes) in order to plan, as best as possible, to either get an idea of how much they will owe or strategies to get a refund as close to zero as possible. You should make adjustments at the beginning of the year, and then have your CPA or accountant revisit them around June 30th to see if you are on track or need to make any changes to the game plan. At tax time, you should not have tax bill surprises or a large refund.

2. Review all pre-tax deductions

There are a handful of tax strategies where you can use pre-tax dollars that will lower your overall tax liability. Based upon your overall cash flow, you should review your 401(k) contributions to determine what you can afford during the year. You may be part of a Flexible Spending Account or Health Savings Account, and should figure out what you can put away pre-tax during the year. If you have a Health Savings Account, you should see if you can maximize your contributions to lower your overall taxable income. You may have other opportunities to buy things like disability insurance pre-tax out of your paycheck. Lastly, if you own a business, there are a multitude of tax deductions that can be taken depending on the structure of the business.

3. Review tax credits
There are many different types of tax credit programs that exist on both a state and a federal level. Doing some investigation about whether you qualify for these credits, or what income level would qualify you for these tax credits, is critical at the beginning of the year. If you are a higher wage/income earner, there are investment tax credits that could lower your overall tax liability for the year ahead. Sometimes, these tax credits are less effective if you buy them at the end of the year versus the beginning of the year.

4. Review your documentation system
Whether you still have the shoebox system or you use a program like Neat Receipts, documentation is key. Since employers are reimbursing less and less for expenses, keeping really good track of your unreimbursed employee expenses will be critical at tax time. In conjunction with your CPA or accountant, you should fully review what expenses can be deducted. Many professionals won't have the time to spend showing you what could be deductible during their busy time – so start asking these questions post-April 15th. Make sure you itemize your non-cash charitable contributions and have receipts for your cash contributions. If you have a side or full-time business, be certain that your personal and business expenses are not commingled. Having separate bank and credit card accounts will allow for the separation of church and state that is necessary to show what is a personal expense and what is a business expense.

The last thing I recommend is to look out at the year ahead and see what changes may affect your overall tax situation. Are you getting married? Will you have a new addition to the family? Are you finalizing a divorce? Are you starting or closing a business? Is there a major purchase you are going to make? Will you be changing jobs? By sitting down with your financial advisor or CPA and having this dialogue, you can put a strategic plan into place for next year. Those who plan end up doing far better than those who wait until they file their taxes to see how the story turns out. At the end of the day, tax planning and tax preparation are two very distinct things. The smart money move for tax management 101 is to plan early and often.

10 Common Mistakes Tax Filers Make

Don't you hate the thought of getting your taxes done only to realize later that you made a common mistake that could cost you time or money? With the tax code seemingly getting more and more complicated every year, here are ten mistakes I see taxpayers make all the time that could put a few extra dollars in your pocket this tax season.

1. If you are single and are caring for an elderly parent, you should investigate seeing if you qualify as "head of household" for your filing status. As a general rule, you should be paying for 50% or more of your elderly parent's expenses in order to qualify.

2. You should make sure you have kept track of your charitable mileage throughout the year. Eligible miles are worth .fourteen cents if you itemized your deductions (this figure is for 2015 – to check other years, visit http://www.irs.gov/Tax-Professionals/Standard-Mileage-Rates).

3. Verify all of the information on your W-2 and/or 1099 is correct. If for some reason the information is inaccurate, notify the issuer immediately so you can get a corrected document.

4. If you worked for more than one employer during the course of the year, you should check how much money you actually paid into Social Security to ensure that you didn't overpay. You should claim a credit for any excess Social Security taxes withheld from your overall wages. We will discuss this in greater detail later in this chapter.

5. If you got a state refund for the prior year, remember that you must include those amounts as income on your federal tax return.

6. If you had expenses during the year such as mileage, meals, and entertainment that were unreimbursed by your employer, consider filling out Form 2106 to see if you can deduct those from your tax return.

7. Make sure to include your Social Security Number on every single page if you file a paper return. This is also true if you have to send in checks to the IRS for monies owed at the end of the tax year.

8. Taking a home office deduction when your employer already has an office for you could trigger trouble. We will discuss the ins and outs of this deduction later in this chapter.

9. Don't ignore the IRS. If they send you documents with questions or about any part of your tax return, make sure you respond to them promptly. Many people believe that it is a good idea to wait for the document for a second or third time. This could cause you undue penalties or interest on money you owe.

10. If your math skills are rusty, many mistakes can be made or opportunities overlooked simply from poor arithmetic. Make sure to use a calculator and double or triple check your math. You would hate to have to answer to the IRS just because of poor addition, subtraction, or multiplication.

Personal Finance 101 -
The Tax Management Triangle

Don't you wish that you had a crystal ball to know what the tax rate will be twenty years from now? According to the Tax Foundation, an independent tax policy research organization, in 1970, the top tax marginal tax rate was at 70%. In 1980, it was still at 70%. In 1990, the top marginal tax rate hit a historic low of 28%. In 2000, that top marginal tax rate had moved back up to 39.6%. In 2010, the top marginal tax rate settled at 35%. With all the uncertainty going on with our debt and taxes, how can you best plan your finances for the certainty of uncertainty when it comes to income taxes?

Over the years, I've adopted a tax triangle methodology around taxes and investing. This allows an individual investor or business owner to think about where they place their investments and tax strategy upon the accumulation and distribution phase. Here are the three sides to the triangle: (1) pre-tax money that will be taxed down the road, (2) after-tax money that will be taxed along the way, and (3) after-tax money that won't be taxed again. Let's talk about these three sides of the triangle in depth.

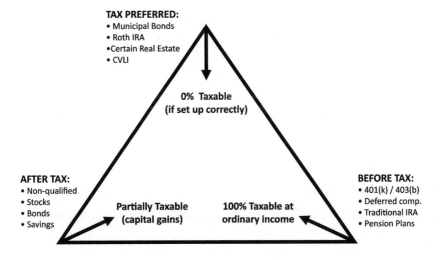

TAX PREFERRED:
• Municipal Bonds
• Roth IRA
•Certain Real Estate
• CVLI

**0% Taxable
(if set up correctly)**

AFTER TAX:
• Non-qualified
• Stocks
• Bonds
• Savings

**Partially Taxable
(capital gains)**

**100% Taxable at
ordinary income**

BEFORE TAX:
• 401(k) / 403(b)
• Deferred comp.
• Traditional IRA
• Pension Plans

1. Money invested pre-tax that will be taxed as ordinary income down the road

This side of the triangle is best imagined as including your 401(k) or 403(b) plan that you invest in through your paycheck at work. The idea of putting money into this side of the triangle is that it reduces your tax liability today, and hopefully you will be in a lower tax-bracket when you distribute money down the road. While the assets are growing, they will increase on a tax-deferred basis so you don't see annual taxation on your tax return. While it does stand to reason that you will have less total income per year when you retire, imagine if you made this decision in 1990 and were now distributing this money at the highest rate today. In retrospect it would not have looked like the best decision. This is why putting all of your eggs in this basket alone will not make sense, but it is important to build up money in this part of the triangle in case this is the cheapest distribution source when you retire. You also need to consider that these assets are mostly tied up until retirement years, as there can be significant taxation and penalties for withdrawing early.

2. Money invested after-tax that will be taxed along the way (and possibly at the time you sell)

Once you have paid income tax on earned income, you may invest those monies in vehicles such as money market accounts, CDs, stocks, bonds, and mutual funds, among others. These investments can generate interest and dividends every year that will add to your overall taxable income. This can also create current taxation on those assets, which could be as high as your marginal income tax rate. This is important to review in both the accumulation and distribution phases. The main issue to keep in mind around the stock/mutual fund-type investments is capital gains. Capital gain rates historically can be very tricky to examine, but they are at an all-time low today – around fifteen percent for the upper income tax bracket taxpayers. They were in the thirty percent range roughly twenty years ago, and even higher before that. In this tax bucket, you need to pay close attention when you sell these assets to ensure you pay the least amount of taxes as you own the asset. In 2013, another change to this part of the triangle emerged from the changes in the tax law with Obamacare, so pay close attention to your trigger point over the next few years.

3. Money invested after-tax that you won't be taxed again in the future

The most recognized vehicle in this asset class is the Roth IRA. Although the Roth IRA was introduced in 1997, it has recently risen in popularity, particularly the Roth 401(k) that has been added to most plans. The reason it is important to add dollars into this part of the tax triangle is that once these assets are taxed, they will never be taxed again as long as they are distributed correctly down the road.

Imagine it is twenty years down the road and you are at the kitchen sink called retirement. The choice at retirement is to figure out which faucet to turn on with your retirement dollars so you can get income with the least amount of taxation. The only way that decision can be made is to accumulate money in different areas during your working income years with the appropriate balance that will afford you the luxury to have enough money in the right parts of the triangle so you can pay the least income tax down the road. The tax triangle is the cornerstone of good tax management; so get started on your triangle today!

Is It Smart to Get a Tax Refund?

Around tax time, I am often asked: "Is it smart to get a tax refund?" The answer really falls into the "it depends" category.

In general, I am not a big fan of getting refunds. In today's world, anytime you give the Government an interest free loan of your money for a year is probably not a good idea. When you get a refund, you withheld too much money out of your paycheck over the course of the year. When your actual tax calculation is done, you will receive the excess withholding back in the form of a refund. This means that you should really sit with your accountant, CPA, or financial advisor to adjust your withholdings for the current tax year (we'll talk about this a bit more in the next section). If you are going to put more money back into your paycheck, make sure you have those dollars systematically saved into some type of savings or investment vehicle so you don't spend it during the year.

Some people like getting that annual refund to pay off credit card bills, do home repairs, or simply take a vacation. It can be seen as a form of forced savings for some individuals, which is where the refund can be a good idea. This is only true if you lack the discipline to save the money during the course of the year. This can easily be resolved by having the money come out of your paycheck automatically.

Generally speaking if you owe more than $1,000 or you get a refund more than $1,000, it is probably time to take a closer look at your tax planning and overall withholding strategy. The idea of good tax planning is to get as close to zero as humanly possible. Even though interest rates are low for most banks right now, you would always rather earn some interest on your money than putting it in the hands of the Government for free for a year.

Get Smart About Your Withholdings

Most people are of two states of mind with respect to their CPA.. they either a) love their CPA because they typically get a big refund, or b) hate their CPA because they owed money. It generally falls into one of those two camps when returns are filed. Remember, if you get a tax refund that means you essentially gave an interest free loan to the

Government. Some people see this as an effective way to force savings during the year, but you really lose out on the opportunity cost of having these resources in your hands during the course of the year.

As of May 2015, the Internal Revenue Service authorized more than 102 million refunds — down a little less than 1 percent from 2014. It also represents more than three-fourths of all the individual income-tax returns processed by the IRS by that date. The total dollar amount of refunds in 2015 was about $274 billion, down slightly less than 1 percent from 2014. The average refund totaled $2,689.

After "tax season" most people tuck away their tax returns, receipts, and other documents and patiently await the next tax season. This is exactly the wrong thing to do. The time immediately following tax season is the exactly the time to sit down with your accountant to look at what is happening this year to adjust your withholdings accordingly so you can tax plan as best as possible.

- *Did you give your accountant your most recent pay stubs to see what level you are withholding taxes this year?*
- *Did you get a bonus this year?*
- *Will you have stock to sell or stock options to exercise this year?*
- *Did you start a business this year or will something change in your business this year in terms of net earnings?*
- *Did you buy or sell a home this year?*
- *Did you move this year?*
- *Did you have a new baby or did you have a baby this year?*
- *Did you get married (or are you going to get married) this year?*
- *Did you get divorced this year?*

Figuring out your withholdings is not an exact science, which is why it is so hard to get the actual refund/owe amount to zero by year-end. However, by asking these questions you can get a much closing sense of what your actual withholdings should be for the tax year. This way you don't have a huge surprise when you file your taxes. By having these dollars in your hands during the course of the year, you'll have a chance to earn interest on your money and possibly save it in different vehicles that are tax-advantaged. Better yet, if you have credit card or other consumer debt to be paid down that can be an effective way to use the money.

If you believe you are so undisciplined that the money you put back in your paycheck from adjusting your withholdings will fly out the door to entertainment or travel expenses, then changing your withholdings altogether may be a bad idea. Each adjustment up or down could mean $1,000 a year or more depending on your tax brackets and overall income.

What to Do If You Find an Extra 6.2% In Your Paycheck

It's pretty amazing how many people still don't understand our payroll tax system. When you work for an employer who must issue a W-2 to you at year's end, both you and your employer are going to pay certain payroll taxes. The two main types of taxes are the Federal Insurance Contributions Act (FICA) tax and the Medicare tax. Both you and your employer pay 6.2% into FICA up to $118,500 in 2015 this year and Medicare is a perpetuity tax at 1.45%.. In 2015, when wages, compensation, and other income streams rise above $200,000 for an individual and $250,000 for a married couple, you will incur incurred an additional .9% Medicare tax. If your W-2 earnings rise above $200,000, your payroll provider through work should be deducting the additional .9% from your paycheck, but it is important you double check at work.

Since there are many individuals who pay their full amount into Social Security and their income exceeds $118,500 in a particular calendar year, unfortunately your HR department won't send you a notice that you now have an extra 6.2% in your paycheck for the rest of the year. This can happen early in the year for those who get large first quarter bonuses or make a big commission check, but for some it will happen toward the end of the year. Surely this money can be saved because you were able to make do without it from the beginning of the year. Here are few ideas of what to do with your extra 6.2% in every paycheck.

- *Max out your 401(k) if you haven't already. In 2015, those under the age of 50 can save up to $18,000 and if you turned 50 this year or are 50 or older you can save up to $24,000.*
- *Pay down consumer debt. If you have any built up credit card debt or automobile loans, start making extra payments and clear out unnecessary nondeductible consumer debt.*
- *Make an extra payment on your mortgage. Doing this every year might actually cut five or more years off the shelf life of your thirty-year mortgage.*
- *Add to your children's college education accounts. Whether you have a 529 plan, UTMA/UGMA, or Education IRA, add some additional monies toward the future cost of college.*
- *Set up a holiday fund. Open an account at your bank or credit union and deposit these extra monies so you don't have credit card debt going into the New Year.*

10 Overlooked Tax Deductions

Much of our time and energy is spent trying to minimize our annual tax bill. Every CPA and accountant seems to have a slightly different slant on the tax code, but here are your smart money moves tips that might help you increase your bottom line and legally decrease your tax bill. Remember to talk with a qualified CPA or Financial Advisor before you decide to implement any of these strategies/deductions.

1. Charitable mileage.

Most taxpayers are very good at keeping receipts of cash donations they make to the organizations during the course of the year. One of the deductions few taxpayers pay attention to is the charitable mileage deduction. If you have charitable mileage to report, remember to include fees and tolls as well. Consider the amount of time that you give gratuitously during the course of the year to your religious organizations, charitable causes you support, or possibly coaching a one of your kid's teams. Consult the IRS for the most up-to-date rules on charitable mileage.

2. Non-cash charitable contributions.

Most taxpayers literally get a blank receipt from the Salvation Army, Goodwill, or other charitable organizations and then tell their accountants that they donated a bag or two for $50. What a huge mistake! The reason you have the blank receipt is to itemize everything you give away line by line to maximize the legitimate deduction. You could go to the Salvation Army's website to find a list of low and high value per item. However, you really need to examine the true fair market value of each item. Make sure you have good documentation and receipts.

3. Form 2106 (unreimbursed employee expenses)

If you look at the number at the bottom of page one of your personal tax return you will see an amount called your adjusted gross income. It is an important number because it sets the bar on other potential deductions you can take. Since employers are reimbursing less and less employee expenses, you should keep very close track of your unreimbursed employee expenses. You must make sure the expenses are for ordinary and necessary items that help you carry on your normal trade. You can see an entire list of possible deductions at on the IRS' website.

4. Know the new tax rates.
You may be thinking about cashing in stock before year end or potentially have the opportunity to defer a bonus to next year. For tax year 2015, for married couples $250,000 AGI, $309,900 adjusted gross income (AGI), and $464,850 AGI are all-important thresholds for the 2015 tax year. If you go over these limits as a married couple$250,000 and 464,850),) you may trigger some potentially damaging additional taxes. This is why you should review your pay stub, triggered stock sales, and much more to be certain you don't get hit for some extra dough.

5. Student loan interest.
A taxpayer can potentially deduct up to $2,500 in student loan interest, regardless of whether or not your itemized your tax deductions. This deduction is often missed after someone graduates from college. The deduction begins phasing out at $65,000 for single filers and $130,000 for joint filers in 2015. Your loan provider will send you a 1098-E form detailing how much interest you've paid for the year, but be sure to take advantage of this deduction.

6. Tuition deductions.
Very often, people don't take advantage of the opportunity to deduct tuition they have paid because they don't understand it. But, it is

possible to deduct up to $4,000 for higher education tuition and qualifying fees. This deduction can apply for tuition you pay for yourself, your spouse or a dependent. The deduction phases out at $80,000 for single filers and $160,000 for joint returns.

7. The charitable IRA.

It's unknown what will happen with this in the future years, but you can give up to $100,000 of your IRA to a charity and avoid paying any taxes on that amount. Far better to potentially gift that away versus using cash, especially for those over 70 ½ who are forced to make a required minimum distribution.

8. Pay your state estimated taxes before December 31st.

If your state has a state income tax, any state income tax you pay during the year is deductible as an itemized deduction on your federal tax return. The fourth quarter estimated installment is typically due on or around January 15 for most states. If additional state income tax payments can benefit you as an itemized deduction, you should get that payment in before the end of the year.

9. Business owners... it's shopping time.

If you have a business, and you anticipate purchasing additional business equipment, consider taking advantage of the bonus depreciation deduction and/or the Section 179 expensing deduction. Equipment includes machinery, computer systems, communication systems, office furnishings, etc.

What If You Don't File Your Taxes?

I am still amazed by how many people call me or come into my office having not filed their taxes for multiple prior years. Some people file for an extension ever year at tax time, while others work feverishly to get them done by April 15th. What happens if you don't file your taxes?

Obviously, we don't ever recommend using this as a strategy. Beyond the interest you will owe for failure to file/failure to pay/underpayment issues, there could be a number of other penalties as well.

- *Criminal fraud – Tax evasion is illegal. I believe that the IRS is going to get even tougher on non-taxpayers in the coming years, and if you are found guilty you could be subject to massive court determined fines, jail time, or possibly both.*

- *Civil fraud - Investors of abusive tax schemes that try to escape their legal tax responsibilities are still liable for taxes, interest, and civil penalties. Violations of the Internal Revenue Code with the intent to evade income taxes may result in a civil fraud penalty or criminal prosecution. Civil fraud can include a penalty of up to 75% of the underpayment of tax attributable to fraud, in addition to the taxes owed. Criminal convictions of promoters and investors may result in fines up to $250,000 and up to five years in prison. If for some reason you don't quite rise to the whole tax evasion issue, you could be subject to civil fraud. According to the IRS, the penalty is seventy-five percent of the portion of the tax underpayment attributable to fraud.*

- *Negligence - The next really difficult question to answer is whether or not you intended to defraud the IRS or really were you just neglecting filing the taxes? In this case, according to the IRS, the penalty is twenty percent of the portion of the underpayments attributable to the negligence.*

- *A frivolous return - Some people think it's cute to be a court jester with the IRS. In these difficult economic times, some taxpayers may protest the IRS by making their job more difficult than it should be. Generally, a frivolous return may omit information that makes it necessary to determine a taxpayer's liability such as their Social Security number. There can be a fine imposed of $500 per frivolous return.*

No matter how many years you are behind, filing taxes is like saving for retirement. It's never too late to start. Get all of your tax documents together, and get yourself down to a good tax preparer to begin sorting through the mess. You have two choices: you can either get them done, or one day you could find yourself doing jail time.

Six Potential Red Flags That Could Get You Audited

Ultimately, you never know what could trigger an audit once this tax season is over. Here are six potential red flags to avoid that could put you in hot water.

1. You make stupid mistakes.

Information has to be entered on a tax return one way or another. If you choose to do your taxes by hand, math errors could be very costly for you in the long run if you get audited. You should consider using a tax program or a professional to avoid making addition, subtraction, multiplication, or division errors. Sometimes, you may miss filling in certain boxes which can be another trigger for the IRS.

2. You have a big mouth.

You should never brag to anyone privately or publicly that you pulled a fast one on the IRS. Especially with the proliferation of sites like Facebook and Twitter, the IRS has become much more intelligent in watching these sites for people who don't report income or try to fraud the Government. Whistleblowers can earn some significant rewards by turning in cheats, so be very careful to whom you share your tax strategies.

3. You didn't file your taxes.

Needless to say that you should file your taxes every year. As I discussed in the previous section, when you don't file your taxes, you could leave yourself open to unwanted penalties and interest. If you don't file for multiple years, you could put yourself in a position to serve jail time as well.

4. You have an unincorporated business (Schedule C Sole Proprietor). Anytime you receive 1099 income during the course of the year, you are in a sense a de facto corporation as a sole proprietor. A business that continues to lose money year after year may be considered a hobby especially if you don't turn a profit over three of the last five years. If the IRS audits you, they could potentially disallow the deductions.

5. You guess on investment cost basis.
No matter what investment company has your money, keeping track of your cost basis is something that you always want to keep an eye on when you do your taxes. This is especially important for people who have inherited individual stock from parents or grandparents and may have inherited the cost basis. While most of the large brokerage firms do a good job of keeping cost basis, many of the direct reinvestment dividend plans don't keep track of cost basis, which may make it a nightmare come tax time. Don't ever try to guess on this as the onus will be on you to prove that you are right.

6. You have a sketchy accountant.
Hopefully you have selected an accountant or accounting firm that is above board. If your accountant promises you a quick refund before your tax return is even completed, that may give you a reason to run for the door. Make sure you are not taking illegal deductions and check everything twice as you will be responsible for penalties and interest if it isn't done right.

Five Tax Mistakes Business Owners Make
Part of putting together an effective tax management strategy is gaining an understanding of what you can and cannot deduct from your

tax return. I see business owners who make mistakes every single day. Here are a few tips that may help you increase your bottom line as you grow your business.

Mistake #1: Having the wrong entity structure.
If you are getting into business for the first time, it's really important to sit down with someone qualified to discuss the way you'll structure your business. The reality is that you can set up your business as a sole proprietor, partnership, Limited Liability Corporation, S-Corporation, C-Corporation, or have multiple structures depending on how many businesses and whether real estate you own will be involved with the business. Since these entities all work slightly different, a huge tax mistake I often see owners make is having the wrong structure for their business.

Mistake #2: Not fully understanding the automobile deductions.
Part of the problem here is that there are many ways to calculate deductions for business use of a car. Here are some brief guidelines that can help you:

- *I'm not generally a big fan of your business owning a car, although different advisors and tax professionals have different views on this. But, you can think about reimbursing yourself for expenses including car payments, as a car allowance would work if you were employed by a larger corporation.*

- *You can take a standard mileage deduction per business mile, or you can take a deduction for actual expenses, including depreciation of the car. But you cannot claim the standard mileage deduction and the depreciation for actual expenses. Be careful about this because sometimes business owners try to take both.*

- *You can switch between these two methods. However, if you go from standard mileage to actual expenses, you cannot take depreciation using the MACRS (modified accelerated cost recovery system) depreciation system. You have to take a straight-line depreciation, which typically yields a smaller initial deduction.*

- *If you decide to have the corporation own the car, 100% of the costs can be deducted. However, any personal use by an employee has to be included as taxable income to the employee. You should review IRS Publication 917 ("Business Use of a Car") to learn more.*

Mistake #3: Missing out on all reimbursable expenses.

Often, business owners will use cash when they are on the road or in some purchasing situation rather than using their business credit card. You should have a detailed sheet of all of your monthly cash expenses used for business purposes so your company can reimburse you. For things like parking, meals and entertainment, or just buying a future prospect a cocktail, you could be losing out on significant money over the course of the year.

Mistake #4: Setting up the wrong retirement plan.

When it comes to setting up the right retirement plan structure, you better be sure you are talking with someone knowledgeable. Since there are a number of programs including SIMPLEs, SEP-IRAs, 401(k)s (with profit sharing), Solo 401(k)s, Defined Benefit plans, Cross Tested Solution plan, and many others, making the right decision about your retirement plan can mean big tax savings to you as owner and will not kill the company's bottom line. For some owners, these plans may allow you to put away more than $100,000 pre-tax depending on the kind of plan, your age, your employee structure, the company cash flow, and what is right in your given situation. I see too many of these plans set up by inexperienced people who don't know how to do the correct analysis and it can have grave financial consequences.

Mistake #5: Not knowing the difference between an independent contractor and an employee.

The IRS is really cracking down on owners who are not specific about the difference between an employee and an independent contractor. Many business owners like the idea of hiring independent contractors specifically because it is less cost to the company in terms of payroll tax, unemployment tax, and potentially a litany of benefits offered by the company. However the IRS has some serious litmus testing you need to examine before you call someone an independent contractor. According to the IRS, here are some factors you should look at when deciding if a worker is an employee or independent contractor.

Facts that provide evidence of the degree of control and independence a worker has falls into three categories:

1. *Behavioral: Does the company control or have the right to control what the worker does and how the worker does his or her job?*

2. *Financial: Are the business aspects of the worker's job controlled by the payer? These include things like how worker is paid, whether expenses are reimbursed, who provides tools/supplies, etc.*

3. *Type of Relationship: Are there written contracts or employee type benefits, including pension plans, insurance, vacation pay, and other employee-like perks? Will the relationship continue and is the work performed a key aspect of the business?*

As a business owner, most of your time is going to be spent thinking about how to drive top line revenue, decrease expenses, and manage your human capital. You should get someone you trust by your side to help you make these complicated tax decisions to maximize your profit and loss statement and increased your overall balance sheet.

The Simplified Home Office Deduction

I have seen a monumental shift to more and more individuals who are freelancers, consultants, or starting some type of home office business over the past five years. The home office deduction has often been bandied about as the dreaded "red flag" that will surely trigger an audit. When you file your taxes, the IRS has offered a simplified version of the home office deduction so you don't have to break out your spreadsheets and start doing a set of massive math calculations.

As of 2015, the optional deduction is $5 for each square foot of home office space up to a maximum of 300 square feet. Instead of filling out the usual 8829 form, you can use a new worksheet in the Schedule C instruction book to enter your simplified home office deduction. Of course, the regular rules around home office deductions will still apply. Whether you are self-employed or an employee of a company, if you use a portion of your home for business, you may be able to take a home office deduction.

Here are six things the IRS wants you to know about the Home Office deduction:

1. Generally, in order to claim a business deduction for your home, you must use part of your home exclusively and regularly:

- *As your principal place of business, or*
- *As a place to meet or deal with patients, clients or customers in the normal course of your business, or*
- *In any connection with your trade or business where the business portion of your home is a separate structure not attached to your home.*

2. For certain storage use, rental use, or daycare-facility use, you are required to use the property regularly but not exclusively.

3. Generally, the amount you can deduct depends on the percentage of your home used for business. Your deduction for certain expenses will be limited if your gross income from your business is less than your total business expenses.

4. There are special rules for qualified daycare providers and for persons storing business inventory or product samples.

5. If you are self-employed, use Form 8829, Expenses for Business Use of Your Home to figure your home office deduction and report those deductions on line 30 of Form 1040 Schedule C, Profit or Loss From Business. But, remember, I previously discussed the simplified option.

6. If you are an employee, additional rules apply for claiming the home office deduction. For example, the regular and exclusive business use must be for the convenience of your employer.

The important thing to note here is that if your employer provides you a desk or a place to work out of at all, you simply cannot claim a home office deduction even if you work out of home more than you do in the office space that is dedicated for you by your employer. Your home office also has to be a separate and distinct space. It can't be a room that is part playroom for the kids and part your office in the corner. In fact, publication 587 specifically gives an example: You are an attorney and use a den in your home to write legal briefs and prepare clients' tax returns. Your family also uses the den for recreation. The den is not used exclusively in your trade or business, so you cannot claim a deduction for the business use of the den. This is a good example for those wondering what kind of room would qualify in your house.

This new simplified home office deduction gives each taxpayer a choice on how to deal with this issue. Avoiding taking a legitimate tax deduction is simply poor tax management planning and furthermore, plain old silly if you really qualify for the write off. The only red flag you have at the end of the day is the one you stick in the ground. No, the movie room/home office won't likely qualify. No, the recreation kids' room/home office won't likely qualify. No, the new kitchen you put in/home office likely won't qualify. Tax deductions like these can often come down to common sense and most of us know the difference. Make sure your home office really is a home office and it could be the best smart money move you make when you file your taxes. If you are really uncertain about square footage, just use the new simplified home office deduction.

Chapter 6

Love, Marriage... and Divorce

What do fairy tales and romantic comedies have in common? They are often concerned with love and marriage (but they are usually not concerned with an important aspect of love and marriage: money).

According to a 2009 study by a professor at Utah State University, couples who disagree about money more than once per month run a thirty to forty percent increase in the risk of divorce. This rate increases with the rate of disagreements. When a couple disagrees (or fights) about money daily, they have a much higher likelihood that they will get divorced –125–160% higher! In this chapter, we'll discuss how to talk about money with your spouse. And, since some relationships just don't work out (perhaps because the couple fought about money) we'll discuss how to manage your financial affairs in event of a divorce.

Seven Smart Money Marriage Tips

You just got married, but you may not have realized that your money did as well. One of you is a spender and one is a saver! How in the world will you make it work? Especially now that many people are getting married in their 30's and 40's for the first time, what should you be doing money wise? Here are seven tips on money strategies for your new marriage.

1. Create separate accounts and one joint account.

To paraphrase Shakespeare, To mingle or not to mingle. That is the question. In fact, it is one of the most important decisions the two of you need to make regarding your finances. On one hand, a couple should have a joint account to manage joint expenses. On the other hand, having your own money to spend however you want can help to lessen arguments about money. I disagree with some experts who say that having separate accounts lessens the sense of unity in marriage and shows a lack of trust in one another. In my view, it can be a way to avoid arguments about spending money on things the other spouse sees as frivolous or extravagant. We will talk about merging finances after you get married in more detail later in this chapter.

2. Track your spending money.

Tracking your spending is not a way to point fingers at one another about who is spending what. Tracking your spending is not having someone looking over your shoulder every time you buy something. Quite the opposite. Having a handle on how much you are spending is critical to achieving financial security. Unless you know where your money is going, it is impossible to set up a budget and work toward the financial goals with which you are both comfortable.

3. Discuss finances together on a regular basis.

Talking about money isn't easy, primarily because money can symbolize different things to each partner. One may view money as security and the other as power. If the topic of debt, bills, savings, and goals makes one or both of you uncomfortable or defensive, seek the help of a financial counselor. It is important that both of you know where you stand financially in order to work toward together your financial goals and achieve long-term stability.

4. Save 10 percent of your income.

Couples living on a "month-to-month" basis, often rationalize that they just don't have enough money to save. But there is almost always money to save, especially if you are adequately (and honestly) tracking your spending. Make the decision to save at least ten percent of your income – no matter what. After saving enough cash as an emergency fund, invest in a retirement account. The earlier the two of you start saving money for your retirement years, the easier it will be have the retirement lifestyle you both hope for.

5. Handle debt as a couple.
Make a plan to pay off existing debt. Drawing a line in the sand and saying that your spouse's debt isn't your problem is not going to work because even if the debt existed before you married, your credit rating can be negatively impacted. In addition, the amount of money the two of you are paying monthly in interest charges can affect your ability to save ten percent of your income.

6. Decide on a bill paying strategy.
Maybe you had a house and your partner had one as well. You were both used to paying your own bills. Now that you are living together and your bills are combined, get clear as a couple on who will pay what bill and which bank account the money is going to come from each month. Having clear expectations will absolutely reduce friction in your relationship over time.

7. Don't keep big financial secrets.
Many people consider not being honest about the cost of large financial purchases — or they keep debts hidden (which is an act of financial infidelity). Such secrets can destroy your marriage.

Should You Buy Your Spouse A Wedding Gift?

A client once asked, "Should I buy my bride a gift on our wedding day?" Weddings have changed so much over the past 20 years ranging from the large-scale traditional weddings to the getaway destination weddings. You've sacrificed to save for a wedding ring that was more expensive than you expected, a party that cost more than you expected it would, and a honeymoon that you had to pay for as well. Is it important to get a wedding gift for your new spouse?

The exciting news is that there aren't many articles out there written by Miss Manners about the dos and don'ts of wedding gifts for your new spouse. It's not necessary that it cost a certain amount of money. Instead, if you buy a gift, it should be something really memorable. This is certainly one of those moments where "from the heart" will mean so much more than from the wallet. Here are a few ideas:

- *Personalized photos of the two of you. What will your new spouse remember two years from now or 20 years from now? The first day you met? Your first vacation together? Your first Christmas together? It's amazing to see photos years later of the two of you when you were just starting out in your relationship. Put it by your bedside or in your family room. It's something your spouse will have forever – and make the frame a special one.*
- *Special piece of jewelry. If you go the jewelry route, I don't recommend spending tons and tons of money. However, it is important to pick out something that you think he or she will wear forever at different times during the year or just a staple that can be worn every day. Think about wht kind of jewelry she or he loves. You might even consider something with her or his birthstone.*
- *First anniversary vacation spot. You could be thinking ahead to your favorite vacation place and book a trip for your first anniversary. This will give both of you something to look forward to one year from now, and it will let your spouse know how much you think about the things she or he loves.*

- *Personalized painting.* *If you love to paint, this can be an incredible gesture. Even if you cannot paint, there are many artists through websites such as www.etsy.com where you can find a painting that won't cost you a fortune. Since you'll be sharing your lives together, consider buying something that has significant meaning.*

Remember that there are no wrong or rights answers with the gift that a spouse will buy for one another. You really just want to let him or her know how much they are loved and how excited you are to spend the rest of your lives together.

Five Smart Money Moves for Getting Married After 40

You almost gave up hope that you would meet Mr. or Ms. Right. However, lightening struck and you finally met the person with whom you are convinced you are meant to spend the rest of your life. At some point, reality sets in as the wedding date gets closer and it starts to dawn on you that there may be real discussions that need to be had around money and financial goals. Not something you typically discuss when you are enjoying fine dining, front row concerts, and swanky hotels on the beach.

Remember, everybody has a financial story – especially the person that you are about to wed. It is important to peel back the artichoke to better understand your partner's attitudes and feelings around money and planning for overall financial goals. Here are five smart financial considerations for those that are getting married for the first time after 40.

1. Should you get a pre-nup?

This is a tricky question, so I'll start by saying that it depends. I am more certain that a pre-nup makes sense if your spouse is coming into the relationship with kids from a prior marriage. This way the assets stay fairly clean on paper. If neither of you have kids or prior baggage, you'll need to have a frank discussion about whether your assets all go into one pot or "what's yours is yours prior to the marriage" and then post-marriage, you build assets together. This is an even more difficult conversation if you have an equity stake in a business.

2. Should you rent the extra house or keep it?

Because you are getting married later in life, both partners may have a home or a condominium, which means you may need to figure out where you are going to live. Let's say your equity is $60,000 net in the other house. If you found that money in your bank account tomorrow, would you go buy a rental property? Will the rental property provide significant tax savings? Do you want to be a landlord? These are questions to ask yourselves as a couple.

3. Who will pay the bills?

When individuals get married later in life, they have generally built up a definite strategy to handle their individual finances. Since both partners have likely been paying their own bills for many years, they should consider who will be the day-to-day CFO of the family finances after wedlock. This can create a much better flow and help with family financial accountability.

4. How will you maintain your financial independence?

One of the most important considerations older newlywed couples need to make is how they will handle maintaining their "personal money independence" while also merging the overall family finances. As we discussed earlier in this chapter, this is a consideration similar to those couples who get married earlier in life. Will you still maintain a separate credit card and checking account so you can buy your partner a birthday gift without them knowing? Will you have one centralized money market account?

5. Kids, kids, kids!

Since you are over the age of 40, the "kids discussion" is a very large rock in the overall financial picture, particularly if there are no children from a prior marriage. If you have kids together, will one of you lose that high paying job? Have you considered all of the free time you have had to yourself for the past fifteen years and what it will mean to have kids? In addition, there are financial instruments outside of the traditional college savings plans that people over 40 should consider because they may turn 59 ½ before the kids go to college or before they graduate.

Getting married later in life presents a unique set of challenges and opportunities. If you ask the right questions and create a mutually agreed upon plan, you'll have much smoother sailing on your life journey together.

Merging Your Finances

When you get married and take your vows, it goes something like this. I take you to be my lawful wife/husband/partner, to have and to hold, for better, for worse, for richer, for poorer, in sickness and health, until death do us part. It does say for richer or poorer. Unfortunately many couples across America just don't spend time discussing money when they get married. More often than not, money can be one of the leading factors that can lead to an ugly divorce.

I believe that the more secretive and separate things are in a financial relationship, the worse it always turns out in the long run. However, merging your finances when you are newly married can be one of the most difficult challenges you'll face after you tie the knot. Merging finances is like merging onto a busy street or highway: you have to do it with caution. What happens if you have more money than your partner/spouse? What happens if your career is blossoming and you bring in more money than they do? Does that give you power and control? Should you change the titles on all of your accounts? Who thought that one of the happiest moments of your life could turn into this kind of mess?

I continue to believe that happiness (or unhappiness) is a byproduct of expectations met (or unmet). Thus, the starting point for merging your family finances is to clearly define roles and expectations. If you can accomplish this as a family, you'll likely have less arguments and disagreements along the way. Here are four important building blocks to consider when you merge the family finances.

1. Independence.

As I've discussed earlier, I believe that each partner will need to have some financial independence. If you choose to have a joint money market account or savings account in which to place the bulk of your cash reserves, it is still important to have separate checking accounts to allow each partner some financial freedom. This will range anywhere from being able to buy birthday and anniversary gifts to being able to treat yourself to something when the time is right. Credit cards can become a more challenging discussion, but having credit cards that are in each of your names is important - especially for establishing and/or maintaining credit. However, no credit card should be hidden (not only because it can create unwanted debt but, it is never a good idea to keep financial secrets from your spouse/partner).

2. Who pays for what?

Who pays the bills (and which ones) is one of the most important discussions for newly married couples. You will need to decide how, if at all, the division of bill-paying labor will be divided. Will each of you have independent basic bills like credit cards or cell phone bills that you jointly decide to just pay and keep in your own name? Without clarity about who plays what role with respect to bill paying, there could be significant ill will every month.

3. Your financial goals.

Take some time to discuss what financial goals are important to the both of you. How much do you both want to have in a cash reserve for an emergency? Do you want to buy a house if you don't have one already? What kind of resources to do you want to save for retirement versus enjoying life today? Are there children from prior marriages, plans to have children together, and college education costs looming down the road? Whether you do this with a financial advisor or within the four walls of your house, this will be one of the major building blocks to getting your finances in order.

4. Your childhood.

Since we all had different upbringings and money experiences, our attitudes about money and what it means to us will be substantially different. Did you take lots of vacations as a family? What was gifting like during the holidays? What kind of birthdays did you have as a child? Did you grow up in a small or a big home as a child? Was there something you always wished your family had bought when you were growing up? These attitudes and thought processes, which we develop over time, shape the way we think about money. It's important to understand how your partner thinks about these money decisions.

There is no real wrong or right way to merge your family finances when you get married. What methodology you use to keep your relationship together is up to you. If you use these four smart money moves for newly married couples, you can set the right expectations to stay happy for many years to come.

Marriage And Medical Insurance

One of the questions I often get is what to do with medical insurance after getting married. Since the medical plans from and financial contributions to individual employers vary, this is an important time in your life to really sit down and analyze the overall situation. This is especially true if both of you have never had kids and are thinking of starting a family within the first year or two your marriage. Here are five points to consider when looking at your plans.

1. True out-of-pocket costs.

The first part of the analysis is for each of you to look at what you truly spent out of pocket over the past year. This includes both the part of the premium that was deducted from your paycheck and the money you spent for co-pay or coinsurance over the past year. You will also want to analyze what would have happened if you were on an employee-plus-spouse plan as well to compare and contrast the "what would have happened" scenario.

2. The network.

Depending on the state in which you live, each plan will have some type of in-network and out-of-network list for doctors within the plan. You should each look at the doctors you are currently using to see which plan may be most beneficial for the widest coverage with the doctors and medical centers you use. There can be a difference in cost depending on whether the plan has a wider or smaller overall network.

3. The deductible and coinsurance.

As you compare and contrast available plans, it is important to look closely at the deductible differences and what percentage coinsurance there is within the in-network doctors. For example, one plan may have a $1,000 individual deductible and a $3,000 per family deductible with 100% coinsurance, and another plan may have the same deductible with an 80% coinsurance benefit (these factors will effect the premium you will have to pay). You may choose to take more risk (by taking a higher deductible) if you want to lower overall cost on your premium.

4. Co-pays.

It is a good idea after examining deductibles and coinsurance to turn to a comparison of of the co-pay you will make for generalist and specialist visits. If you have to go to the doctor regularly, a $20 per visit difference can put a dent in your budget – the affect can accumulate over the course of a year.

5. HRA or HSA.

One final item is to determine if your employer has a healthcare spending account (HSA) or a health reimbursement agreement (HRA) plan (both could potentially lower your premiums). Over the next several years, you will likely see the HRA become more popular as small business owners try to mitigate their risk by offering a reimbursement to employees (this is especially important as you use your own money to meet the plan deductible). If you don't get sick and use the funds set aside for you, it gives the business owner the chance to keep their expenses with respect to maintaining health insurance for the business.

Obviously, the other major consideration will come if you have a pregnancy within the first year of marriage, even with the new healthcare insurance rules. Be sure to closely analyze which health insurance coverage option is best for you. It could end up being better to have the family under a single plan or actually separate members between two plans based upon the overall net cost to you. Health insurance used to be a simple and easy decision, but with the complexity of plans and multitude of choices, it is important to review this as a family or with a qualified financial advisor.

Update Your Beneficiary Designations

Today, many people are experiencing significant and sometimes sweeping changes in their family situations. Perhaps a recent divorce, separation, or marriage. Or, perhaps your children have moved out or have a new relationship of their own. Maybe someone in your family recently passed away. Changes in any type of family situation could be a very important trigger to review your beneficiary designations.

The U.S. Supreme Court emphasized this point in the 2009 Kennedy v. DuPont Savings and Investment Plan case. In that case, a spouse, divorced in 1994, was awarded all rights to her ex-husband's retirement plan benefits (in a dispute with his daughter) even though the ex-wife had waived all claims to the benefits in the divorce decree. The problem is that prior to the death of her ex-husband in 2001, he had failed to change the beneficiary named in the plan documents. Thus, all of his retirement benefits (approximately $400,000) went to his ex, and none to his daughter. Ouch. Talk about unintended consequences!

Even though you may update your will and make changes, your beneficiary designations will override what you put in that will. In order to ensure the smooth transition of your assets, you should consider having both a primary and a contingent beneficiary designation. Review these designations annually as you review your overall financial plan as well as when your overall financial picture changes.

Can Your Family Live on One Income?

As families grow and careers take off, many couples are faced with the whether or not one partner can/should leave the traditional workplace to care for children, particularly when factoring in the cost of childcare. Here are three things you should consider when deciding on whether or not a family living on one income is a smart money move.

1. Treat this analysis like a business decision.

Every business has three main parts to the profit and loss statement: income, taxes, and expenses. When you are considering a big family financial decision, such as transitioning to a one-income family, what you are trying to compare is how much net income you are going to lose against how much expenses (and time) you are going to save. Let's leave benefits aside for the beginning part of the analysis. If your spouse makes $50,000 per year, will it reduce your overall tax bracket with less income in the next year? How much real net income do they bring into the family business? What type of expenses will disappear when your spouse no longer has to go to work? If you spend the time to create a detailed breakdown of your family income and expenses, you should be able to find whether the job loss will be a net positive or negative after your spouse quits their job?

2. Assess your overall benefits situation.

If each spouse in the family gets a corporate benefits package, typically some of the benefits will run through one spouse and some of the benefits will run through the other. The key benefit to assess is health insurance (in order to determine if the working spouse's health insurance is adequate enough for your family if you lose the other spouse's health insurance). Will it cost your family more money?

Will you have to change your primary care physician because of she or he is not in-network for the spouse who will be provided health insurance for the family? Will you lose your HSA or FSA opportunities? In addition, if the spouse quitting work has low-cost life insurance or disability insurance, there might be other expenses that should factor into the overall cost benefit analysis.

3. How will bills get paid?

One of the interesting social shifts today is that more and more people are getting married later in their working careers. This is typically the time where each partner has built up some assets, but more importantly is used to having the independence and sole task of managing their own checking account. If one spouse stops working outside the home, it is important to have a family discussion about how the stay-at-home spouse will access cash if they need it for basic expenses. You should also determine who is going to pay the bills and how the division of labor will be divided between the working and stay-at-home spouse so there is no built-up resentment. This is the time to get clear about expectations.

Deciding whether you will be a family with one or two working spouses is an incredibly tough decision – no matter how many kids you have. Some people make the transition to one working spouse when they have their very first child. Others eventually transition after the birth of their third child when it feels more like zone defense than playing man-to-man defense. Consider the pros and cons to make sure you go through a thorough analysis so you can make the smartest money move for your bottom line.

Who Will Take Care Of Mom and Dad?

Many Gen Xers are probably beginning to see the early stages of their parents slowing down or perhaps one of them has had a mild health scare over the last five years that got you thinking: "Who is going to take of Mom and Dad?" Before each one of your brothers and sisters rush to put their finger on their nose and scream "NOT IT!," it may be time to have a serious discussion about who will bear the responsibility should your Mom and Dad need someone by their side for financial or medical decisions.

Gen Xers has literally been ripped apart from a location perspective when it comes to family as they chased high-paying corporate jobs, an increased divorce rate, and the search for potentially better locations in which to live. The days of everyone living right down the road is a distant sight in the rear view mirror. Here are a few key thoughts you should consider as a family when you ultimately sit down for this discussion.

1. Who is going to be the leader of the pack?
It's actually pretty rare in my experience to see all brothers and sisters get along when it comes to the how to take care of Mom and Dad.   Siblings typically have varying opinions on things like in-home care vs. a nursing home, advanced medical directives, and financial matters. Practically speaking, one brother or sister needs to be the point guard for making decisions. Sometimes, one sibling will step into this role by default because they live closest to Mom and Dad or they are the one who is most financially responsible. Mom and Dad may have made their own appointments in their wills or trusts, but you should still have the discussion amongst yourselves especially if nobody lives close to Mom and Dad.

2. Are we going to contribute any money?
Most parents won't reveal their entire financial situation to their kids. However, you may decide as brothers and sisters to pitch in and pay for a long-term care policy in order to make sure your parents

receive quality care and to potentially preserve their estate. If you are thinking as a family that you may keep the original family house or a subsequent vacation property, you might want to have some discussion on who will put money in the pot to have maintenance and upkeep of these properties. What if there are outstanding debts to pay? All of these types of questions are important ones to cover in the discussion.

3. What if one sibling wants out?

We know that life is stressful and there is an increased strain with geographic separation for brothers and sisters to retain close relationships.   What happens if one sibling is in jail? What happens if one of them struggles with addiction? What happens if one of them just says, "No thanks," and the rest of the siblings are left to deal with the situation. But if one sibling wants out, the remaining one(s) still need to build a game plan no matter what. You don't want to run into a situation where nobody knows what is going on when the time comes that Mom and Dad need your support.

4. Do we have the skillset to give mom and dad care?

Initially, many siblings will try to figure out who can work part-time, who can help before or after work, and who can help handle the daily living activities Mom and Dad may not be able to accomplish on their own. You need to seriously talk as a family and try to decide if you have the emotional and professional skills to really be a part-time or full-time caregiver. This can be difficult emotionally especially if your Mom or Dad has a degenerating disease.

As children, sometimes we may be unable or unwilling to help with caring for Mom or Dad. You should be very careful because it is easy to get resentful that your life has changed because you are the responsible one. Opportunities may arise (things that you might have to give up if you are the one responsible for Mom and Dad), and relationships among brothers and sisters can become strained. By sitting down as a family unit and really have a thorough discussion on this topic, you can save a lot of that heartache down the road. Gen Xers probably thought that this subject was many years away, but the truth is that it's right around the corner.

Six Things To Do Before You Get Divorced

Divorce is never an easy thing to go through, no matter what time in life. The trauma that it may create for you, your children, and other family members may push day-to-day financial decisions fall to the bottom of the pile. Many people wait to try to get their financial house in order after they complete the divorce proceedings. Having seen people go through divorces over the past 20 years, I've come up with six important things you should do before you get divorced. By making these smart money moves, you can get your new financial situation off to the right start and not be left with tons of nagging financial problems from the divorce.

1. Watch spending and keep debt down.

Most of the time, the discretionary cash flow you have in your personal situation will tend to decrease after the divorce due to child support or decreased personal income. Since your financial situation is going to change, you can begin the change process by limiting your discretionary spending immediately. If you can, pay down any debts held solely in your name. When it comes to debt, you may want to be sure your lines of credit are open especially after a divorce. Often, one spouse stops building up their own credit and that can hurt them down the road.

2. Obtain your and your spouse's credit reports.

Do you have access to credit in your name alone? If not, then begin to establish credit cards in your name only. This may also include opening bank accounts and a brokerage account. Obtaining a credit report is important because your spouse (soon to be ex) may be out racking up tens of thousands of dollars of debt that could become your responsibility when the divorce happens. Take a snapshot of the debt you have now and keep track of it until the divorce is final. When taking this snapshot, be sure to include all of the accounts - people often don't realize how many financial instruments they hold jointly. Also, be certain that you can access those cards online or over the phone as the lead person on the card could change who has access to those accounts. What you don't want to have happen is for your credit to get ruined during the period of time before you get divorced.

3. If you own a business, get it valued.

When it comes to items like a business or land, often the values can be abstract. Your soon-to-be ex may ask for a piece of the business, a salary, or just a portion of the current value of the business today. It's important for you to take the lead and establish a value of the business today certified by a CPA. This may cost you a few bucks, but it could potentially save you big money down the road. Many business owners bury expenses within their business that a spouse may not know about, which is why the valuation can be tricky when it comes to divorce purposes. If you own land, then consider having a market appraisal done so you can create a fair valuation of that land today as well.

4. Make copies of all financial records and statements.

If you don't already have this done (or set up in a software program or online service), you should quickly make a list of all assets and liabilities. Try to find out: Are there retirement accounts you don't know about? Are there accounts for the kid's college education? Are you certain you know of every bank account that exists? Make a list of all account numbers, titles on accounts, balances, financial institutions, automobiles, household items, etc. When the assets get split, you certainly don't want to have a surprise after the fact.

5. Examine all beneficiary designations.

Over the course of time you were married, on some of your accounts you may have been required to name a beneficiary. This could include insurance policies, annuities, IRA's, 401(k), and other financial instruments. Any accounts that are owned by your spouse can have a beneficiary change made without your approval with the exception of some 401(k) plans, which will require a sign off. It's important to know who is designated as beneficiary on these accounts as this could potentially be discussed throughout the divorce proceedings.

6. Prepare for legal costs.

Most people will fool themselves into thinking that things will work out amicably until money, kids, and new relationships begin to unfold. Prepare for legal bills that could range from thousands to potentially tens of thousands of dollars depending on how ugly the divorce proceedings get. Some people spend money hiring a private investigator before the divorce to make sure there is no monkey business going on or to reveal other facts that may be important to the overall split of the assets. You should also be prepared that even after the divorce, there may be other legal costs should your situation or your ex's change in the future.

When divorce happens, it can set off a gamut of emotions. These six tips are a reminder that without a lot of planning your divorce may never have a happy financial ending. Making these smart money moves can help you figure out how to secure and maintain your own financial independence in the event of a divorce.

What Can Tom Cruise and Katie Holmes Teach Us About Divorce?

We all know divorce can be a costly process no matter your financial situation. Think back on the breakup of Tom Cruise and Katie Holmes – the Paparazzi were buzzing about how much it would cost Mr. Mission Impossible to make the divorce possible (although it should be noted that Katie Holmes had amassed considerable wealth and celebrity status on her own, but the bottom line is that divorce can be a messy process). So what smart money moves can we learn from the third divorce Tom Cruise is went through with Katie Holmes? Here are four financial ideas to potentially help you if you have to go through separating your assets in a divorce.

1. Try to minimize legal fees.

If you and your ex can maintain a reasonably amicable relationship, you could save more than fifty percent of your legal costs by doing a collaborative divorce. This type of process means you won't have to have rabid lawyers sitting across the table from each other (this process uses cooperation rather than confrontation). If this doesn't work, then you could look at mediation before you get the high-powered attorney batting it out for you while they decrease your net worth by the hour.

2. Keep a low profile.

Even though divorce can cost a lot of money, maintaining a relatively low profile can keep your overall costs down. Even if you aren't a movie star, you don't want to put yourself in a position where your social media accounts can allow lawyers to dig up damaging information that can cost you even more money. Getting a confidentiality clause can be a good idea so information after the fact doesn't hit the local media.

3. Discuss your real estate options.

Real estate can be one of the trickiest items to discuss when going through a divorce. Whether you own one home or multiple homes, you need to take a close look to see whether your home(s) are under water or if there can actually be money made on the sale of a home. Since exes generally want to start fresh and get into new living spaces, the cost of selling one home and potentially buying two new ones can really decrease the overall net worth of your family. It's important to have cooler heads prevail and think about the short- and long-term ramifications of home value, school systems (if kids are involved), moving costs, and other potential ancillary expenses.

4. Maintain the right insurance.

It's important to discuss how much life insurance each spouse will have on each other after the divorce. I recommend that each spouse is the owner of the policy on their ex so they can be sure it can't be changed and premiums are paid. This is often overlooked because there is so much focus on the asset base, but each spouse should want life insurance in place especially if there could be a second (or third) marriage down the road. A close examination of the health insurance situation should happen as well to ensure the kids are on the best possible medical coverage depending on which spouse carried the health insurance.

We see high profile stories every day in Hollywood waiting to hear about the large settlements such as the Mel Gibson case where he lost half of his reported $850 million dollar net worth. We aren't all as lucky to have that type of wealth, so it's important you start grasping some of the new rules of divorce. These smart money moves may help you if this situation happens to you at some point in your life.

Chapter 7

Managing the Rising Cost of College

For many couples, after love and marriage, comes the baby carriage. And once a couple has children, it's time to start thinking about paying for that child's education (especially college). In this chapter, we're going to discuss the important considerations to make with respect to college education planning. We'll start with some widely held assumptions and then talk about common mistakes, the basics of college planning, the pros and cons of various college savings vehicles and some unusual places to look for scholarships to help foot the bill for college. Ready? Let's go!

What Are Your Assumptions?

You get home from work one day and your child has the magical letter to open from that college or university that you both always dreamed she or he would attend. It's possible the school is your alma mater or perhaps the acceptance letter is from the Ivy League university you always hoped your child would attend. As you open the letter, you read that your child has been accepted into the new freshmen class, but you soon begin to realize that maybe you haven't done your homework to pay for his or her college education. Let's examine some of the key areas you need to be thinking about when you plan for this type of financial goal.

Many financial plans often use blanket assumptions – this is not always a good idea. When you start thinking about college education planning, it is important to have a lengthy discussion with your financial advisor about what you want the picture to look like so you can backtrack into the right assumptions. College is getting more expensive, but it is never too late to start planning for your kid's future. The good news is that you have more options than ever before to start saving for this important goal. What are the key assumptions you should be thinking about for college education?

1. How do you plan to finance the college education?
Essentially, there are four options you could consider about how you assume you will assist in paying for your child's college education. You could pay as you go, although this is not recommended. This means assuming that your job will generate the kind of future cash flow you need in order to add college tuition as another bill. You could choose to pay later, which means borrowing or financing your kid's education like a mortgage and paying it off over time. This could hamper other goals you have, like paying off your mortgage or early retirement. You could find someone else to pay, which could be a combination of relatives, financial aid, grants, scholarships, etc., which can be viable if you plan skillfully. The last thing you can do is to save for the goal, which requires important planning and discipline to reach the goal. This question is vital in building a foundation for your overall strategy.

2. What do you think the rate of inflation is going to be for college costs?
The cost of college education continues to increase because of a number of factors including states decreasing funding for education, a decrease in endowments and donations, and an increase in the number and caliber of buildings and facilities on campus that might attract new students. According to the College Board, the ten-year historical rate of tuition increase at private colleges is approximately

six percent – almost twice the normal inflation rate during the last decade. If your financial plan uses a normalized inflation rate, this could substantially skew the projected numbers you need to save for college versus the actual money you will need to save. These numbers also don't include other costs your child might have like: housing, living expenses, computers, supplies, books, and transportation. Many people don't factor in these ancillary expenses when they put their plan together.

3. How much of the education do you plan to fund?

According to SavingforCollege.com, a child enrolling into a private university in 2015 can expect the total cost for tuition to be about $134,600. If the inflation rate stays at six percent this number will be over $350,000 for a child born today. So the real questions to determine when you have a new baby are, "How much of the education do you plan to fund? Do you want to plan for a public education or a private education? Do you want to fund two years or all four years? Do you just want to give your child a head start?" Answering these questions provides you with a really good baseline to understand your starting point.

4. Can you expect any family help?

Although this can be a difficult conversation to have with your parents or grandparents, it is a very meaningful one so you can plan for your child's future. Be sure to ask what support, if any, you can expect to get from family members. This isn't a selfish or greedy question. It is vital to know this so you can plan to save your kid's investments into the right type of vehicles for tax savings and liquidity depending on what the rest of your family may be doing. Sometimes parents or grandparents want to help, but they do not know the most effective way to save money while retaining control of the assets.

You may now realize that every puzzle is going to look a little different for every family. Your particular circumstances, number of children, overall asset base, income level, and many other factors will help determine the best strategy for your family. But the first step is to sit down and put a plan together – just like you would for anything else you have successfully planned. Wouldn't it be great for your child to open that letter, and you have the power to know that you planned well for that magical day?

The Timer Is Winding Down For College Education

When saving for college, remember it is important to pull back on the risk in the investments. In the last big market downturn, many parents got hurt because the funds they saved for college were nearly cut in half when the stock market dropped by fifty percent. Just as it is important to diversify your own portfolio, it is equally important to diversify the way you save for a child's college education.

Beyond savings, also consider ways to fill the gap between what already has been saved toward a kid's college education, and what it will cost between tuition, room, board, fees, and other ancillary expenses. While all of us can only hope our child wins an academic or athletic scholarship, it is best to plan conservatively and design a strategy to save or borrow to pay for the college education.

If you have never heard the term FAFSA, then chances are you will at some point soon. FAFSA stands for Free Application for Federal Student Aid and this will be the form that determines what type of monies you may be eligible for to supplement your own college education savings. Available at fafsa.ed.gov, the form should be filled out regardless of how much (or how little) income a family has. One of the biggest missed opportunities occurs when parents, often erroneously, think they have too much income for their student to be eligible for grants or student loans. There are major differences between federal student loans and private student loans, which are important to know.

What is a federal student loan? A federal student loan allows students and their parents to borrow money to help pay for college through loan programs supported by the federal government. They usually have low interest rates and offer attractive repayment terms, benefits and options. Generally, repayment of a federal loan does not begin until six months after the student leaves school. Federal student loans can be used to pay school expenses such as tuition and fees, room and board, books, supplies and transportation. Federal student loans are delivered to students through the Direct Loan Program. Loan funds are provided to you through your school.

What is a private student loan? A private student loan is a nonfederal loan issued by a lender such as a bank or credit union. Private student loans often have variable interest rates, require a credit check and do not provide the benefits of federal student loans. \

Why are federal student loans a better option for paying for college? Federal student loans offer borrowers many benefits not typically found in private loans. These include low fixed interest rates, income-based repayment plans, loan forgiveness and deferment (postponement) options, including deferment of loan payments when a student returns to school. For these reasons, students and parents should always exhaust federal student loan options before considering a private loan.

As I mentioned earlier, most people may believe that filling out the FAFSA form is not a worthwhile exercise because they make too much money or have more than ample resources in the bank. I think it is important to go through the process to find out if a particular school is participating and whether or not funds are available. It is important that you get your FAFSA form in as early as possible. January 1st typically kicks off the FAFSA season and some states have deadlines as early as February 15th. State deadlines are found at www.fafsa.ed.gov. Also prepare to estimate income even if the tax returns are not complete, and make certain to know which assets should be included and which will not. These can all have an effect on how much federal student aid granted.

The real determination of aid will come from a calculation called the Expected Family Contribution (EFC). The EFC is the number that will actually be processed on your FAFSA form. There are three separate worksheets for the EFC formula, so make sure to use the right one when completing the paperwork. A big decision will be do you fill out the dependent student form or will you use the independent student form? At the end of the day, the lower the score, the better chance of federal student aid.

Top Ten College Planning Mistakes
1. No overall game plan.
Many clients I sit down with have not done a realistic plan or projection of what the real cost of college education is going to be for their children. With today's software, you can actually go college by college (in-state vs. out-of-state) to calculate the cost of college education. Are you looking at private school? Public school? In-state? Out-of-state? Inflation adjustment? All of these are just a sampling of questions to help you figure out how much it is going to cost for college education, how much you need to save today, and what after-tax rate of return your money is going to need to earn to help you reach the goals you plan to achieve to give your children

financial support. www.savingforcollege.com is just one website to go through this type of exercise.

2. Choosing the right college savings account.
There are many different vehicles today for saving money for college education. Once you have built an overall game plan within your financial plan, you should have a better idea on exactly which college savings plan makes sense for you. Should you take out the popular 529 plan? Is it a good idea to get a Coverdell Education Savings Account (ESA)? Perhaps taking a look at the notion of doing an UGMA or an UTMA? There are various other methods including Savings Bonds, Roth IRA's, and Life Insurance. You need to clearly look at the tax ramifications of each plan, cost, investment choices, and more to determine which one is right for you. Making the wrong decision here can be a disastrous mistake. We will take a closer look at these different types of vehicles later in this chapter.

3. Not matching your investments to your time horizon.
Most people we meet for the first time truly don't understand how their money is being invested for their children's education. More importantly, a big mistake I see is a failure to match the time frame of those investments to the type of investment where the money is located. A great example of this is seeing parents whose child is going to college in one year, yet 100% of the money is still invested in the stock market. Many parents felt this pain a few years ago when the stock market crashed, and are now having to experience finding other alternatives on where to come up with money to pay for college. As a child's high school graduation draws closer, the overall balance of stocks and bonds should become more conservative. If you don't have an appropriate time frame, (I recommend at least five years) you may not want to consider utilizing the stock market to achieve college education saving because of the risks involved.

4. Underestimating inflation of college tuition.

Inflation rates have historically hovered around three percent. However, as I discussed earlier in this chapter, college education costs have been in the five to six percent range, which is double the normal inflation rate. This means the cost of college will literally double every twelve years! This is where you may want to consider plans such as Prepaid Tuition Plans or other vehicles that may allow you to keep pace with rising inflation. You need to carefully consider the pros and cons of these plans, but this is a major miscalculation when most parents do goal-setting for college education saving.

5. Using your retirement account to pay for college.

It is a big mistake to sacrifice your retirement for your kid's college education. It can become even more of a financial wreck if you get involved in taking loans from your 401(k) plan or other type(s) of retirement plans. This can cause a major hiccup in the time value of money in your own retirement account, and it can be very difficult to recover in the later years of your life. More importantly, while paying for a child's college education might be a worthy goal, borrowing against your retirement savings might mean you have to adjust your vision of retirement, living on less money or working longer than originally hoped.

6. Raising the expected family contribution.

With so many concurrent financial responsibilities hitting around the same time as most kids are hearing off to college, it is important to keep a close eye on the calculations around the expected family contribution (EFC). The EFC really concerns how much of your income and savings you'll need to spend before financial aid will kick in for your student. Seeing where your income is going to be, how assets are titled, and what other assets you are going to sell are serious considerations around these calculations. Make sure you understand what counts for your name and your child's name when it comes to what assets you will have available for use for college.

7. Not researching grants, scholarships, and loans.
Your child doesn't have to have a 4.0 GPA or be a star athlete to qualify for free money! Scholarships are based on a variety of criteria and can be found on the Internet, in scholarship guides, and through sponsoring groups. Some of these scholarships can be obscure, but every dollar counts when it comes to paying for a child's education. The key is to stay organized during the scholarship search by keeping a list with deadlines and requirements. Make sure you and your child research all avenues from all areas that touch your life. If you can't apply online, be sure to leave enough time to request, complete, and mail a hard copy. Also, be sure to build in time to request letters of recommendation for those applications that require them. A good starting point is the website www.college-scholarships.com, but your local schools and libraries are also great resources. In addition, your child's guidance counselor can be a great resource.

8. Not managing the cost of investing .
This mistake is true of all of your investing decisions. However, because the time frame you have to save for college education is often shorter than the one you have for retirement, you need to watch your costs even closer. When you choose investments for college education, make sure you analyze all the costs that you may not see in an investment including trading costs, management fees, 12b-1 expenses, operating expenses, and custodial fees. Especially when it comes to 529 plans, you can determine the fees associated with the overall plan, which may help you decide whether the in-state plan makes the most sense, the out-of -state plan, or using an independent plan works best for your situation. It is a good idea to talk to a financial advisor or a CPA before making the final 529 decision. A one percent

saving in cost over an eighteen-year time frame can make a dramatic difference in the amount you have to save.

9. File FAFSA annually in January and research your eligibility for federal and state aid.

Two-thirds of all full-time undergraduate students receive some kind of financial aid, so odds are your child is eligible, too. The federal government has a formula that determines the amount your family is expected to contribute to your college costs. Any costs above that have a chance to be covered by financial aid. The Free Application for Federal Student Aid (FAFSA) is required to be considered for federal student aid. The FAFSA may be required by colleges, state agencies, and some scholarships. Complete the FAFSA for the first time as early as you can during the spring semester of your senior year of high school and every year thereafter that you are in college. The new FAFSA form is updated and available each year in January, and the sooner you apply, the better your chances are to receive the maximum amount of financial aid for which you are eligible.

10. Not setting realistic expectations with your kids.

No matter which path you set out with respect to your kid's college education, be realistic about what is affordable in your family budget. You should also be clear about whether your child will have to get a job while going to school, how much, if any, spending money you will be able to provide, and what your household can afford overall. While a four-year private school may be the dream school for your child, the cost of a four-year public school may be what your budget can afford. Make sure your child knows what you can realistically help them out with so they can plan their future for the next four years. The more clearly you set expectations, the better the journey will be in college.

A Vacation or College Education?

I have noticed that some Gen Xers spend too much money on vacations and not enough saving for college education. "Where should we take the kids for spring break this year?" "Even though the children have sports and camps over the summer, wouldn't it be nice to have a memorable week away at the beach?" Have you ever asked these types of questions? In fact, there is a good chance that you spend more time planning that picturesque vacation than you do thinking about what it will cost for your kid's college education.

Generation X parents spend a great deal of time thinking about the vacations they want to take. However, one of the big mistakes seen among Generation X parents is that they spend very little time planning out the overall cost of these vacations. Any trip for a family of four (where you aren't able to use frequent flier miles/reward points) that involves airfare, hotel, car rental, and food/entertainment for a week is going to be in the $3,000 to $5,000 range. If you take two of those trips during the course of the year, you are potentially looking at $10,000 a year of erosion to your bottom line.

The reason this discussion is so important is that if you have two children, the cost of a private school education can be in excess of $200,000 if you are planning to fully fund that college education. Even for a public in-state school, it can cost you in the $50,000 to $75,000 range depending on your state and the institution. If you have just one fourth grader and have not started saving yet, it will take you saving more than $5,000 a year just to get close to paying for an in-state public college education. (Based on six percent inflation for college costs, and a seven percent investment return).

Most Gen X parents want to be able to do it all for their children while balancing that with having fun for themselves. This means having a wonderful home to grow up in, traveling to some cool vacation destinations, and wearing brand-name clothes. However, you need to plan to have some balance between saving and spending when it comes to vacations and college education or you just might wind up taking a left turn to destination nowhere.

What Types Of Savings Vehicles Can You Use?

The next step in successfully planning for a child's college education is determining which of the myriad savings vehicles will best help you achieve your goal. Since the tax laws are different from state to state, I recommend you consult a financial advisor and/or a CPA before you make any final decisions as each of vehicles we are going to discuss in this section have tax and/or control implications down the road. Here are few types of options that you may consider when investing your lump sum or monthly savings.

1. 529 plan or prepaid plan.

529 plans are usually where there are the most questions about college planning. Essentially, 529 plans are a way to save after-tax dollars into a vehicle that will grow tax-deferred. In addition, 529 plans allow you to withdraw the money tax-free for your child's college education. It is important to compare available plans, state by state, to determine the potential tax ramifications and advantages. Most brokers/financial advisors won't sell you the in-state plan, as some of those plans don't generate commission, so they will sell you out-of-state, commission-producing plans. Additionally, since the beneficiary can be changed from one child to another, I am a proponent of putting more money in your first child's name as the unused savings can be transferred to the next child. Last, many of these plans have a finite number of investment choices so you will have to watch performance closely to hit your goals.

2. Uniform Gifts to Minor Act/Uniform Transfer to Minor Act (UGMA/UTMA).

In this type of college education savings account, you are making a "gift" in your child's name. This means when they hit your state's majority age, the money in the UGMA/UTMA will technically become their money. This feature can make parent's feel shaky about investing in a UGMA/UTMA account. However, these accounts offer a lot more flexibility than many 529 plans; you can set up a UGMA or UTMA at most major brokerage houses, insurance companies, and banks. In addition, you get a small tax break through these accounts with something called the "kiddie tax." This means that the first $950 of interest/dividends earned on the account is tax-free and the next $950 of interest/dividends earned on the account is taxed at the child's rate.

3. Savings bonds.

As a kid, getting a Savings Bond from your grandmother left you wondering, "What am I going to do with these?" Most of us just ended up putting them in an envelope in our sock drawer or in a safety deposit box in the bank until we actually remembered we had them. Savings bonds can be an easy way to save for a child's college education because many employers will allow you to directly deduct them from your paycheck. However, the rules have become more stringent with respect to how you can use the Savings Bonds tax-free for college education. They can only be used for tuition, and the income limitation phase-outs are fairly low. One good thing about these bonds is that they work on a set interest rate. This can be beneficial if you want to take the uncertainty of the stock market out of the college planning mix.

4. Coverdell Education Savings Account (ESA).

One final vehicle to mention is a Coverdell ESA. Essentially, this vehicle allows you to put post-tax dollars into an account that will grow tax-deferred and can be pulled out tax-free for any type of education. Since 529 plans are dedicated for college expenses only, the Coverdell ESA (and the UGMA) gives parents the ability to save money for goals such as private elementary, middle school, and/or high school. Like an IRA, you can save the money in any type of investment instrument allowed within an IRA. However, Coverdell ESAs limit the amount you can contribute per year, so it won't get you too far if you have big savings goals.

You may have figured out that picking the right type of college savings vehicle requires homework. You need to determine if one or a combination of these savings vehicles is the right strategy for accumulation and distribution of your child's college funds. Your particular circumstances, number of children, overall asset base, income level, and many other factors will help determine the best strategy for your family situation and goals.

Choosing the Right College Savings Plan

As college costs for both private and public schools continue to escalate, so does the confusion around what type of college savings plan to choose. Many families make the mistake today of only using a 529 plan, which can be a big mistake. Consider how much money is needed, when you will be distributing the money, and how to balance savings plans and vehicles between children.

The following table summarizes and compares the features of 529 plans, ESAs, and UGMA/UTMAs.

YEAR 2015 RULES	529 Plan	Coverdell Education Savings Accounts	UGMA/UTMA
Federal Income Tax	Non-deductible contributions; withdrawn earnings excluded from income to extent of qualified higher education expenses	Non-deductible contributions; withdrawn earnings excluded from income to extent of qualified higher education expenses and qualified K-12 expenses also excluded	Earnings and gains taxed to minor; first $1000 of unearned income is tax exempt; unearned income over $2,000 for certain children through age 23 is taxed at parents rate
Federal Gift Tax Treatment	Contributions treated as completed gifts; apply $14,000 annual exclusion, or up to $70,000 with 5-year election	Contributions treated as completed gifts; apply $14,000 annual exclusion	Transfers treated as completed gift; apply $14,000 annual gift exclusion
Federal Estate Tax Treatment	Value removed from donor's gross estate; partial inclusion for death during a 5-year election period	Value removed from donor's gross estate	Value removed from donor's gross estate unless donor remains as custodian

YEAR 2015 RULES	529 Plan	Coverdell Education Savings Accounts	UGMA/UTMA
Maximum Investment	Established by the program; many in excess of $300,000 per beneficiary	$2,000 per beneficiary per year combined from all sources	No limit
Qualified Expenses	Tuition, fees, books, supplies, equipment, special needs; room and board for minimum half-time students	Tuition, fees, books, supplies, equipment, special needs; room and board for minimum half-time students; additional categories of K-12 expenses	No restrictions
Able to Change Beneficiary	Yes, to another member of the beneficiary's family	Yes, to another member of the beneficiary's family	No; represents an irrevocable gift to the child
Time/Age Restrictions	None unless imposed by the program	Contributions before beneficiary reaches age 18; use of account by age 30	Custodianship terminates when minor reaches age established under state law (generally 18 or 21)

YEAR 2015 RULES	529 Plan	Coverdell Education Savings Accounts	UGMA/UTMA
Income Restrictions	None	Ability to contribute phases out for incomes between $190,000 and $220,000 (joint filers) or $95,000 and $110,000 (single)	None
Federal Financial Aid	Counted as asset of parent if owner is parent or dependent student	Counted as asset of parent if owner is parent or dependent student	Counted as student's asset
Investments	Menu of investment strategies as developed by the program	Broad range of securities and certain other investments	As permitted under state laws
Use for Nonqualifying Expenses	Withdrawn earnings subject to federal tax and 10% penalty	Withdrawn earnings subject to federal tax and 10% penalty	Funds must be used for benefit of the minor

College Education Or Entrepreneurship?

Generation X parents continue to face the challenge of climbing uphill to save for their children's college education. For a Generation X couple that had their first child in 2015 the estimated cost of a private college education is more than $340,000. As crazy as that sounds, a parent would have to save over $1,150 $1,085 per month in today's dollars to be able to reach that goal. For most parents, the thought of saving that much money to pay for the cost of education for just ONE child can be downright daunting. The cost of a college education cannot defy gravity forever, but to this point there has been no stopping the rising costs for a four-year degree.

During the formidable teenage years, many parents help guide their children toward getting excellent grades in school, playing some sort of athletic sports, and filling their resume with extracurricular activities. However, parents and educators do not place much emphasis on helping young adults focus their energies on becoming early stage entrepreneurs – and that could be a real benefit as the years unfold.

Sean Belnick started his business when he was fourteen. Before office retailers like Staples started bringing their businesses online, Belnick saw a huge, untapped market for furniture back in 2001. So he aimed to simplify the process consumers faced of buying furniture by founding BizChair.com. He started small, initially selling only office chairs. By selling goods directly to buyers, Sean managed to rake in revenues of $42 million by 2008. He has since expanded the business to include more furniture for offices, homes and restaurants. Now, at age 25, he continues to lead the firm's evolving market strategy and to focus on the development of new IT initiatives. In 2010, Belnick, the parent company of BizChair.com, saw sales rise to $58 million.

Always on the hunt for new ideas, Ritik Malhotra began programming when he was just eight years old. Four years later, he started a website that let viewers read comics online, and after reading up on useful SEO tactics, he managed to attract 250,000 visitors in one year. He eventually mastered the art of making websites, starting a gaming site and then a popular web forum that attracted 6.5 million viewers in a single year. Following that, he ran a webhosting and software consultancy business called HostingAxis by the time he was thirteen years old. It garnered a return of more than 600 times his initial investment. While the site had revenues in the high single-digit thousands, Ritik shut it down just before he entered high school so he could focus on his studies. Now, Ritik is co-founder of Silicon Valley Prep, a learning academy that teaches various levels of competitive math, computer science and public speaking to elementary, middle, and high school students. A 2012 Thiel Fellow, the nineteen-year-old also co-founded Greply, a venture-backed startup in Silicon Valley, and built a tool that allows users to search the web for the cheapest deals on any given product. Revenues from Silicon Valley Prep have totaled up to $45,000 in one summer alone.

These are just a few stories from the thousands of young entrepreneurs in America today. With the ease of access to technology, everyone can encourage kids to be creative and think about a new business or idea that can become a business. It would be interesting to put twenty kids side-by-side and give them each $518,000. One of them would use it to start a new business and not go to college. One of them would use the money to earn a four-year degree at a good college institution. Twenty years later, who do you think would be more successful?

Are Private Colleges Worth The Price Of Admission?

College education and health insurance costs are two areas that have defied gravity. With college tuition escalating at a much faster rate than normal inflation and thus continuing to press on family savings, the average household may wonder if getting a diploma from an expensive prestigious private college is worth the cost of admission.

If your son or daughter is lucky enough to have the qualifications to get into the ultra-elite schools (such as Harvard), then my answer is yes. There is a short list of impressive schools that have a strong alumni base stretched out across the United States or have the really high end credentials necessary to help a student make a major impact with their career in the short term.

There are many very good private colleges that cost $50,000 to $60,000 a year beyond the short list of these prestigious schools, and they may not be worth the money, especially if you don't live in the geographic area where the school is located.

In the state of Georgia, both Georgia and Georgia Tech are ranked in the top 100 schools within the United States. Not only are these excellent schools, but if you plan to live in the state of Georgia, their alumni base will be stronger and more beneficial than a prestigious private college located halfway across the country. Often, in-state colleges can be a much better bang for the buck than a private out-of-state college, especially if you plan to work locally after you finish your education.

Business experience tells me that 'who you know' will always trump 'what you know,' so consider that in your final analysis if you plan to write a big check for a private college education for your child(ren). It will be hard to find definitive statistics on this topic, but going to an elite private institution will likely be worth the price of tuition.

Top Ten Unusual Scholarships

Searching for possible scholarships, grants, and financial aid can be a daunting task. As I mentioned earlier in this chapter, the Free Application of Federal Student Aid (FAFSA) application should be your first stop, but there are many other sources to uncover additional monies to help supplement the cost of college. Here are ten unusual scholarships that you may want to consider to help finance your child's education.

1. The Milk Mustache Scholarship.

We know milk does a body good, but how about your wallet? Every year there is an award called the Scholar Athlete Milk Mustache Of The Year Scholarship. You will need at least a 3.20 GPA just to jump over the bar to get in the nomination process. Winners can get up to a $7,500 scholarship.

2. Skater boys.

Well, really it doesn't matter if you are a boy or a girl. Just have a minimum of a 2.5 GPA, and let these folks know how skateboarding has had a positive impact in your life. You could be eligible as a grand prize-winner for up to $5,000 in scholarship money. Who says it doesn't pay to be like Tony Hawk?

3. Be tall or be short.

It just doesn't pay to be average in stature anymore. There are scholarships given just for men who are above 6' 2" and women above 5' 10" and for people who are shorter than 4' 10". The Billy Barty Foundation offers scholarships for those who are short, and the Tall Clubs International Scholarship has awards for those who are tall.

4. I've got the best apple pie.

The Culinary Institute of America offers a $25,000 scholarship to the winner of its All-American Apple Pie Recipe Contest. Applications must include an original apple pie recipe, a photograph of the finished pie, a 500-word essay about apples, a high school and/or college transcript, and an application for The CIA's bachelor's degree program with supporting documentation. That may be more grueling than an episode of Chopped!

5. I want a Duct Tape dress at the prom.

Duck® brand duct tape offers a $5,000 scholarship for the lucky couple who can use their brains to make the most unique prom outfit using Duck® brand duct tape.

6. Star Trek Convention.

This scholarship is open to people who want to study language. Offered by The Klingon Language Institute, the scholarship is $500.

7. Make better cotton candy.

The American Association of Candy Technologists awards up to a $5,000 scholarship for a sophomore, junior, or senior who has demonstrated an interest in confectionary technology.

8. The hangover.

Tylenol offers scholarships in various amounts.

9. Green Eggs and Ham.

The Dr. Seuss story Oh, the Places You'll Go offers a $10,000 scholarship for the person who can inspire Dr. Seuss with an original two-dimensional art piece reflecting the meaning of Oh, The Places You'll Go.

10. Seinfeld.

Jerry Seinfeld established this scholarship that offers up to $10,000 to cover the costs of college education. This scholarship is only open to those who graduate from a New York City high school.

Three Smart Financial Gifts For The College Graduate

I was recently a guest on CNN Headline News with Lynn Smith to talk about what kind of gifts to give the college graduate. In my opinion, it is too common for families and friends to give senseless gifts – whether they have the means to do so or not. So, here are three smart financial gifts to consider for the college graduate.

Get a budget! youneedabudget.com.

Do you still want the kids to be living at home until they are 30 years-old? If the answer is no, then you need to consider teaching them the #1 financial skill in life that is most certainly not taught in college: how to manage a budget. Ultimately, they need to learn the real cost for day-to-day fixed expense, discretionary expenses, taxes, and saving so they can take care of themselves. For $60, you can get the college graduate in your life on the road to a more stable financial future.

Open a Roth IRA.

How important is it to start saving young? You can run the math, but a 22 year-old who saves $2,000 a year into an IRA until they are 30 vs. a 30 year-old who saves $2,000 a year in an IRA until they are the age of 65... the 22 year-old will always have more money irrespective of interest rate. Remember, the college graduate must have earned income in order to be able to open a Roth IRA.

One year of LinkedIn Premium for job seekers.

Remember, in life it's not necessarily what you know, it's who you know that will matter. The résumé of the college graduate will have higher visibility with premium and they will also be able to send InMails, which can help them toward securing a new job.

Graduation can be an exciting time for families, but it should also be a time where you don't lose sight of helping your new graduate make smart financial moves. Paying off their student loan debt would be the ultimate gift, but it may not be in the cards. Consider these smart money moves to say Congrats!

Chapter 8

10 Smart Money Moves for Entrepreneurs

Many people dream of starting their own business and being their own boss. While there are many success stories told about people starting businesses with little or no money and earning millions, the road is littered with far more entrepreneurs who have had far less success. In this chapter, I am going to discuss 10 lessons about entrepreneurship. These lessons are a mix of lessons I've learned in my more than 20 years as a business owner coupled with observations I've made working with and advising new business owners. So, let's jump in and get you on the path to that business you've always dreamed of starting.

Lesson #1: Being Undercapitalized

It's always exciting to think about the idea of starting your own business. You've heard stories where entrepreneurs started with just $300 and a cardboard box and then turned their business into millions – heck, we even told a few of these stories in Chapter 7. In reality, having worked with many types of business owners, the first mistake made by most is simply not having enough capital or access to capital while growing your business.

Undercapitalization means not being able to sufficiently fund a business venture. An idea alone will not lead to business success. This lack of capitalization is not only concerned with the initial outlay to get the business up and going. To fully capitalize your business, you need to as honestly as possible calculate the business' operating expenses, especially in the first year of operation.

Here are three smart money moves to think about so your new entrepreneurial venture doesn't fall short financially:

1. Lines Of Credit.

You should have a written, documented line of credit that you can access should the business need capital. This line of credit can be from a bank or a network of family and friends. If you do not have lines of credit in this way, do you have credit cards available with lines of credit ready to go if you have no other access to capital? You could also try places like www.lendingclub.com or www.propser.com if you can't gain access form normal channels for credit. But the bottom line is this: you have to have available lines of credit in order to account for unexpected business expenses.

2. Up Your Pro Forma By 50%.

Whatever you project the cost to run your business in the first year of operation, it would be smart to add 50% to that number. We often cut twice and measure once in the first year of running a business rather than measure twice and cut once.

3. Lease vs. Buy.

Many banks will work out a 3 or 5-year $1 buyout program on equipment, which may allow you to use your upfront capital more effectively in the first year of business. If you can stretch a line of credit or do an equipment lease it may be a good idea versus using your cash that may otherwise strap the business' resources.

Many businesses fail in the first year primarily because they run out of money. Make sure you don't fall in the trap by being undercapitalized!

Lesson #2: Incorrectly Pricing Your Product Or Service

In the first year of a start up operation, the new business owner typically focuses much of his or her energy on client acquisition. Winning new customers opens the floodgates for the generation of revenue to pay the business' bills. However, one of the tough lessons learned by young owners is not thinking clearly though pricing the business' goods and services correctly.

Most new business owners tend to undervalue what they charge for their work and services in order to compensate for not being as established as their competitors. As long as you have a top-notch customer service experience and offer a product or service that's similar or better than a competitor, you shouldn't devalue yourself. If you set this pattern early, it can be difficult to raise your prices with your initial customers down the road.

Here a few tips that may help you determine if the price is right on your new product or service:

1. Shop The Competition.

As part of a new entrepreneurial venture, you should be doing some research about what kind of competition you have locally and on the internet. Take stock of where your competitors have set the market rate, and place your prices relative to the value you believe you can deliver in the market place.

2. Beta Test Your Top 5.

If you know five people who will likely buy your product or service, consider throwing a consider running a beta test with them or what they call an A/B test to determine your pricing structure. Gaining some valuable feedback from these customers could prove to be instrumental in bringing more like customers down the road.

3. Offer Options.

Having several options for customers, including being able to pay annually, monthly, by credit card or PayPal, or slight variations of choices will allow more new customers to determine the price that is right for them. Be careful about just picking one price point at the initial phase of the business.

Many businesses fail in the first year because they incorrectly price their product or service. Make sure you focus on getting the price right!

Lesson #3: Know Your Role As The Owner

As an entrepreneur starting a new business, you often have to wear the hat of cook, dishwasher, accountant, and general manager. However, one of the biggest mistakes a new owner will make is failing to clarify his or her role within the organization. Far too often, new entrepreneurs will try to control every aspect of a new business, which inevitably slows the growth of the organization. In some cases, it can make hiring and training new people so difficult that it can be destructive to the success of a company.

One of things I recommend to new business owners is to draw a T chart with one axis being things you like to do and one access being tasks that you are good at currently. What you should quickly try to figure out in the early stages of a new company is a list of all the things you are good at and those tasks you like to do. After figuring out this critical piece of analysis, you should begin to try to surround yourself with others who you trust enough to delegate the things you aren't good at and you don't like to do.

Here a few tips to consider when trying to figure out what your role is as the owner of a start up:

1. Your Passion.

With the thousands of successful business owners I have known and worked with over the years, the very best of entrepreneurs are the ones who define their role by their passion. If you are excited about what you are doing every day, the people you hire that work for you will feel that energy through the organization until it becomes infectious.

2. Your Skills.

You have had both formal schooling as well as informal training through odd jobs over your life. Think about the courses in school that you excelled at and why you did very well in those classes. Think about the jobs where you wanted to work overtime because you loved what you were doing and you were successful in the tasks that were given to you. It is important that you maximize your strengths.

3. Your Vision.

Your role within your new entrepreneurial venture should always be focused around the bulls-eye of your company. If you had a target to shoot at with a bulls-eye in the middle, what words or goals would be written on that bulls-eye? It is important that your energy be focused on the things that drive the vision of where you want to be in 1, 3, or 5 years.

Many owners try to be a jack-of-all-trades and sink the ship on their new company by not focusing on what matters most. Know your role!

Lesson #4: Avoid Rookie Mistakes

We're not professional athletes. However, we would imagine that the rookie year on any of the professional sports circuits has to be daunting. Not only are you performing in front of a large crowd, you also have to get used to all of the decisions you have to make to be the best of the best in what you do for a living. Far too often, new entrepreneurs can make first year decisions that can put a major dent in the inaugural year of a new entrepreneurial venture. Even someone who has a lot of corporate experience cannot understand the firefight of being a business owner until he or she has to meet her or his first payroll.

One great idea I have put into place in my business is the 48-hour rule. I've set criteria around what a "key" decision is for my business and once I have made a decision on the direction I want to go, I, along with my team, revisit the decision in 48 hours to confirm that it is still, in fact, the right decision. Here are few areas in which you should implement this rule so you don't have rookie mistakes harm your first year in business:

1. Decisions over a certain dollar amount.
Whether the amount is $1,000, $5,000, or $50,000, you really need to look closely at your pro forma (profit and loss statement), and consider what dollar amount, if spent incorrectly, could derail your business venture. If you have any type of financial decision above your set dollar amount, take those 48 hours to challenge your thinking process on why you are making the business and financial decision you are about to make. If it still makes rational sense after waiting 48 hours, then you can pull the trigger. Almost all of your big decisions can stomach the 48-hour time frame.

2. Technology.

Whether it is buying computers, cell phones, servers, or a phone system, you will have many different technology decisions to make in your first year in business. Remember that the people you ask for advice will typically have different opinions based upon the products they sell or the framework of technology they prefer to use. This is a great opportunity to gather both opinion and fact to cross-reference in order to make what you think to be the very best decision. Since technology changes so fast, you don't want to waste first year money making incorrect technology decisions.

3. Staffing.

Make sure you have a set process on how you will find the employees you hire. Many new entrepreneurs make the mistake of hiring new employees they really like (and are like them), rather than placing the best person strategically into the role. It is best if you can have written criteria around your interview process and in some cases have an internal or external personal screen the candidates. Most importantly, ASK and CHECK the references someone gives you, even if you are in a rush to hire for a new position.

Many owners get so excited about their new product or service that they end up making rookie mistakes many of us have made before. By planning thoughtfully you won't be able to avoid all of these. However, if you can avoid a few of these rookie mistakes, your new business can be even more successful in the first year.

Lesson #5: You Must Hire Professional Consultants

Since many new entrepreneurial ventures are started on a shoestring budget, where you spend your financial resources can be a prickly situation. Far too often, new business owners are really penny wise but pound foolish, as the old adage goes. When is the right time to get legal help? Do you really need an outside person to manage your books or can you do it yourself? Does your business merit having a financial person to talk to about entity planning and business structure? Can't you just figure this stuff out yourself?

Even with many years of corporate experience, I faced these same questions when I opened my business. The cost for some of these professionals feels like a waste of money when you need those precious resources for things like marketing, staffing, and technology. However, a big mistake in any of the areas we'll talk about below can be a brutal blow to business growth. Here are a few areas we would not go without in your new business:

1. Legal.
In my business, I have worked with over 1,000 business owners. Many of them still remain unprotected in areas of their business because they didn't spend the money to get the right kind of legal help. If you are creating products or services (including blogs) that need trademarks, patents, and/or copyrights, you need to protect what you are building. In addition, a good lawyer can help you with your employment contracts, non-competes, or non-disclosure agreements as you hire new employees and pitch your ideas. If you have any notions of tying employees in with stock options, a legal advisor can be even more important as a first year consultant in your business.

2. Financial/Accounting Help.
Based upon whether your business is more capital or service intensive, a good financial advisor and/or accountant can help you determine the right structure/entity for your business. If you set up the business incorrectly, it could cost you thousands of dollars in missed tax opportunities, as we discussed in Chapter 5. You should get someone to handle your books as the banks today will really want to

see you have all of your ducks in a row when you come asking for money (or refinancing debt) down the road. These professionals may also be able to help you with your pro forma, overall company forecasting, and/or shopping bills in your business to get the best deal.

3. Human Resources.
Most entrepreneurs open a business and hope to get away from the human resources department they knew at "big" corporations. Since each state's laws, policies and procedures vary, having a human resources consultant is critical so you can learn the dos and don'ts about your work place environment. They can help you set an initial policy handbook for new employees or advise you about what you need to have in place if you hire a bunch of independent contractors. The last thing you want in your first year in business is a lawsuit from a terminated or disgruntled employee.

Spending $5,000 or $10,000 for these type of consultants feels painful when you become a new entrepreneur and are strapped for cash. It will always seem like these people are overpaid and underworked when you write the checks. However, it is to get these people in place to protect you as your business grows.

Lesson #6: Poor Staffing Decisions
One of the mantras of management is "you have to put the right talent on the bus." While I understood its meaning, it took many years to realize how important hiring decisions are to grow an organization the right way. I have felt the pain of making poor hiring decisions, and how much time and productivity you can lose from just one bad hire. No entrepreneur lives in the panacea of having zero turnover, but making the right staffing decisions by putting people in the right roles can allow

your start up venture to scale quickly. The wrong staffing decisions can leave your new company mired in constant, unplanned change.

One of the critical questions to ask early in your venture is what role do you (the CEO/owner) play in the firm. In what jobs will you act as a "player" versus those where you will act as a coach? What jobs will lie somewhere between those roles? The first thing for you to figure out is what your role is going to be, and that makes the process of making the right staffing decisions a lot easier. Here are three points to consider avoiding making poor staffing decisions:

1. Hiring family members.
This can certainly be a double-edged sword as there have obviously been many successful family businesses over the years. However, it is important to determine if the family member you are hiring has the skills necessary for the position. While you may potentially get some more immediate loyalty and buy in from a family member, it can also be a lot harder to separate ties should that person not be able to adequately fulfill their obligations within the job. You should be certain that you compare and contrast multiple candidates before you make a quick decision to hire a family member because it is "easier."

2. No set interviewing process.
Let's face it; résumés are somewhat of an art form today. It's really hard to rely on a one-page document that is probably more processed than Velveeta cheese. You should have a series of interviews (with more than just you) designed to learn more about the candidate personally and professionally. One of the early mistakes new entrepreneurs make is they gloss over checking references. A really good candidate should have willing work and personal references who will speak on their behalf so you can validate the quality of the candidate. If a candidate cannot give you references to validate their work and credentials,

then this is the type of candidate you should avoid hiring in your business. Make sure you run each candidate through some type of technology test as almost all interviewees put down that they know how to do PowerPoint, Excel, etc., but few really know these programs.

3. Have a dating period.
One of the most important lessons I learned as an entrepreneur is to fail fast. You cannot succeed quickly as an entrepreneur without failing, but you must do it fast. Don't hire a new candidate full time until you have some sort of 90-day trial period. During that dating phase, your level of difficulty and scrutiny should be as high as humanly possible. You don't want to become "buddy buddy" with your new employee as this will set things off on the wrong path. You should be certain to test every aspect of the candidate's job after they have passed your interview process to make sure this is the right person to have a seat on your company's bus. Otherwise, you've only lost 90 days – or less – if it doesn't work out.

Many owners make the big mistake of falling in love with a potential new employee because their "personalities" mesh in the interview process. Don't be fooled by some initial chemistry. Instead, focus on a thorough job interview process. This will save you time and money down the road.

Lesson #7: Milking The Business
Before deciding to open my own business, I spent over 10 years in senior management. While I garnered a ton of personal and professional growth and experience over the years, nothing really prepared me for being the CEO of my own company. However, I learned a lot about Profit and Loss statements and the importance of managing to the bottom line.

If you have worked for a corporation for a few years before starting your own venture, you need to really prepare to not have a paycheck every two weeks. While you hear stories about all the personal things that your business can pay for through the company, milking your company can be a very big problem. If you start to build the mentality that the company can pay for just about anything because it is a write off, you could end up having substantial problems meeting payroll, debtors, or hitting the bottom line targets you are aiming for. So how do you avoid milking the company?

1. Decide on the right level of cash reserve.
Although your accountant might like the fact that interest rates are really cheap and tell you to draw down your business account to zero, I like the idea of having a cash reserve just like you would have in your personal life. While I recognize that business accounts don't earn any interest, as your company becomes profitable it makes sense to sacrifice some personal income to build up between three and six months of your monthly expenses into your business cash reserve (separate from your personal cash reserve). By doing this, it will build some discipline to only draw what you really need to live on until the company has bigger and better profitability.

2. Make a pro forma for the year.
As hard as you try, it's going to be nearly impossible to know every single expense that will hit the business in the start-up phase. There will be some legal, technology, and/or staffing bill that will pop up at some point. However, by creating a pro forma in the beginning of the year, you can clearly make a demarcation line for which bills you will try to run through the business and which will remain personal. Remember, when you burden the business with more expenses, it is also a reflection on how you make some of your growth decisions.

Try to make the pro forma by adding only discretionary expenses that make sense for the business in the initial stages.

3. Create a check and balance system.

It's important to have someone else work on your books. If you don't have a set of books, you have officially uncovered your first problem. Having an outside third party or an internal partner/employee act as some sort of check and balance system is a good idea. Think about it this way: If you are the judge and jury on all of the financial decisions, what do you think is going to happen in a time where you need money or want to buy something for yourself?

Whether you are in the initial stages of business or your company is becoming profitable, milking your company for your own benefit can be one of the main reasons your company crashes to the ground. This is especially true if you allow your lifestyle to match the company growth. Then, suddenly (like we saw in real estate) the market makes a correction in your particular industry. If you avoid milking the company from the beginning, you'll have a better framework for you and employees of your organization.

Lesson #8: The Marketing Plan

Marketing your products and services is the lifeblood of any new business. While you can ultimately have all kinds of long-term business strategies, without having a steady stream of new revenue your new business venture can close in a short period of time. In my opinion, if you look at the three areas of business including 1) marketing, 2) the actual product or service you are offering, and 3) client service, marketing is the one driver that can help sustain a business —even if the other two areas are slightly subpar. There are really two parts to the marketing plan. One section involves dealing with implementing strategies that will specifically drive new client acquisition.

The other arena is building the brand of your new company.

Many new entrepreneurs substantially underestimate the time and money it will take successfully market a product or service. Your networking functions, community involvement, and meeting face-to-face with new prospects about your product or service will chew up a significant amount of time in your week. In addition, you'll have to be mindful about how you and your employees keep a level of consistency about the core message of the company. Here are three mistakes to avoid in your first year:

1. No tracking system.
You could throw whatever you want against a wall and see if it sticks. This might work in the short-term, but it is not an effective way to market long-term. Any marketing expenditures need to be tracked. Specifically, you are trying to figure out what each lead cost you for a given marketing campaign, what your lead conversion is on each lead source, and what your ultimate return on investment is by lead source. This will help you make more effective short- and long-term marketing decisions as you spend resources within your company.

2. Go narrow versus wide.
In some ways, the show on television called the Deadliest Catch can teach you a bunch about marketing. Nobody really has the money to dump an unlimited amount of traps around the entire ocean floor. It would be way too costly to do this (and many marketers try to do it this way). You need to think about having 2 or 3 really good marketing traps, but based upon your best demographic and psychographic data, pick a part in the ocean where you think you can get your best return for dropping the traps.

3. Ask the question why?

One huge mistake marketers make in a new venture is to try something once and never again. Many companies execute a direct mail campaign once, and because no leads were generated as a result of the campaign, they assume direct mail won't work. Instead of having that attitude, ask yourself the following questions. What were the results from the campaign? What happened? Why did this happen? How would changing the variables be more effective the second time around? What key learnings influence the marketing strategy going forward? By creating a new hypothesis, it will get you closer and closer to the bull's-eye - more new clients. Without asking why, you will bounce from new marketing idea to new marketing idea without improving result.

My company has had huge success in marketing. Every aspect of your marketing plan starts from day one: from your business cards to your voice mail message and web site. Make sure that you spend enough time considering all of these aspects or your new business will be open and shut in less than a year.

Lesson #9: Execution

I remember the Executive Vice President of a Fortune 500 company at which I was working saying, "Execution is the one thing that separates the good from the great. Let me put it to you this way. If you don't execute, you'll be executed." We guess it's hard to forget that, but it still rings true today. Some of the best leaders and managers in business don't achieve peak results because they simply don't execute the plan.

If you like to read, I highly recommend that you pick up a book written by Larry Bossidy and Ram Charan called Execution. There is a wealth of knowledge in this book about execution, and how to be successful at getting things done. Here are three mistakes new entrepreneurs make when it comes to execution:

1. Changing the plan too often.
One of the sayings I love is that focus beats brilliance all the time. In your first year of business, it is easy to get distracted by five more new money-making ideas that you see as ventures that can put additional dollars in your pocket. The problem is that if you lose focus on your business plan, it can confuse your employees, potential investors, and even you as the owner. As hard as it will be to uphold this, in the initial stages of your business try to refrain from changing the game plan you laid out for you and your employees. It will create a bottleneck in achieving flawless execution of your game plan.

2. No benchmarks and review process.
Since the first year of the business will fly past in the blink of an eye, it is crucial to have a dashboard for the major metrics you are trying to achieve. Whether this is a gross revenue number or a certain amount of new clients, it is important to have a score card so you can, on a daily or weekly basis, see how you are doing against your plan. In an effort to decide how to channel your time, energy, and financial resources, this dashboard and regular review process will allow you to make the best decision on where to execute. Then, you can step back (or you and your management team) and decide the best way to execute. Most businesses utilize something called the Key Performance Indicators (KPI) to determine the health of the business and the best way to execute financial and human resources. It's up to you to determine those key indicators, but I would recommend keeping it to three so you can narrow down your daily focus with your team.

3. Poor communication.

Since you are the visionary of your business, it is easy to connect your actions against what you envision as the end goal. However, day-to-day, it can be difficult for employees to understand the "why" behind what they are doing because they cannot connect the dots. You need to make sure you are overtly clear about linking the strategies you are putting in place against the vision on where you see the company going in one, three, or five years. One of the biggest mistakes new entrepreneurs make is poorly communicating this to their employees and investors. This can be a big problem in trying to execute your main initiatives in the first year.

During the first couple of years in business, you will constantly be challenged with the bicycle pedals of motivation and discipline. When motivation weans, discipline must kick in to keep the bicycle moving. I have always felt that those best at executing a game plan manage to have incredible discipline doing the things that have to be done even when they don't want to do them. Execution is all about that analogy. Stay disciplined against your strategy and only turn the bicycle when it needs to be turned or you'll end up with a flat tire.

Lesson #10: Passion, Persistence, and Perseverance

Lessons one through nine were extracted from my own business and other business owners across the country with whom I've worked over the past twenty years. Undoubtedly in your first year of business, you will make your fair share of mistakes - like anyone starting a new business venture. There are so many valuable pieces of wisdom to learn as an entrepreneur, but here are our big three traits you must have to truly succeed in your business.

1. Passion.

Many business ventures people conjure up in their heads often revolve around the dreams of making a lot of money. While building your wealth can be an outcome of a successful entrepreneurial pursuit, passion around your dreams is what will get you through the good times as well as the bad times. When you get out of bed every day with positive emotions about what you are doing, it becomes easy to motivate others to get excited around that dream. Imagine if your business made you no money at all. Would you still have the passion to get up every day and do what you do?

2. Persistence.

You ask 10 people to invest money in your new business and they all say no. You complete a week's worth of sales and marketing calls and everyone doesn't want to buy your product or service. You have two employees quit in the same week and now have to answer the phones yourself. These are examples of things that will make you feel like you got kicked in the stomach. Your ambition, drive, and persistence to stay focused on the key tasks when adversity hits you will keep you on track to reach your goals.

3. Perseverance.

The legend goes that Colonel Sanders was reduced to living off of just $105 of his Social Security check as he began his venture to make the best fried chicken the world. He supposedly made over 1,000 calls to different restaurants and bars having people try his fried chicken until he perfected the recipe. Just remember that as a new entrepreneur (especially if you have a college degree): most people will tell you that you are crazy, stupid, and/or out of your mind. No matter what anyone tells you, if you persevere through all the criticism you will find that pot of gold at the end of the rainbow.

I think our future lies in the dreams of those who start their careers as entrepreneurs and take the road less traveled. Enjoy the journey and dream big!

Chapter 9

Protecting Your Family Today and Tomorrow

We're now at the "not-so-fun" part of the book, where we have to discuss insurance and estate planning. While arguably, thinking about budgeting, debt, taxes and investing was not really that much fun, we now have to start thinking about getting older, and the inevitability that we will die at some point. In this chapter, we're going to talk about how to determine if you have enough insurances to really care for your loved ones when you pass away. In addition, we'll talk about strategies for ensuring your estate is properly structured.

Why $1 Million Is Not Enough Life Insurance

Having been a practitioner involved with life insurance more than 20 years, I've unfortunately had to deliver a fair share of insurance checks. When I meet people who have lost a loved one and now have to build a financial plan, never once have they said, "Boy, I'm so angry my life insurance agent sold me too much insurance!" Rather, I hear horror stories from widows and widowers who cannot understand why their partner didn't take out more life insurance. Or, they were assured they would be "well taken care of" if anything happened to their spouse. This is the story for many families across America.

I've recently seen both friends and family members who are between 40 and 45 years-old dealing with major medical issues. Three different people I know drove themselves to the emergency room thinking they might be having a stroke or heart attack. Three others were diagnosed with various forms of cancer. I also know of two separate cases where friends have been diagnosed with diabetes. In your 20ss, you never really had to worry about this kind of stuff. In your 30's you start to feel it a little bit here and there. But, in your 40's is where you start to see some of the more major stuff. So, now is the time to start planning!

When it comes to life insurance, most people use some magical rule of thumb like buying 2 to 3 times their salary. Even worse, since insurance is not the most enjoyable financial planning topic, they come up with the notion that they will just pick up $250,000 or $500,000 and their partner will be alright if something should happen to them. I'm here to tell you that when it comes to life insurance, even $1,000,000 isn't a lot of insurance.

First of all, at today's guaranteed interest rates, $1,000,000 will barely generate $10,000 per year of income if you don't want to touch principal. More realistically, it may only generate $40,000 to $50,000 if you use a diversified bond portfolio. However, if you go that route there is no guarantee that your principal won't fluctuate. Usually when someone passes away, liabilities have to be paid off. If $250,000 is left on the mortgage, credit card debt, final and funeral expenses, and potentially putting away for your kid's college education, you can blow through $1,000,000 quickly. And here is one more thought for you: if you are 35 years old and buy $500,000 of life insurance for a 30 year term, about 20 years into that term (assuming inflation is 3%), the $500,000 will actually be only worth $250,000 in terms of real money. Few people think about the impact of inflation on their insurance proceeds when buying life insurance.

Here are three tips to ensure you have enough life insurance:

1. Whatever amount you come up with initially, boost it higher.
A lot of Gen Xers get their term insurance coverage through their jobs, and I think the trends show that many of them will change jobs many times before they reach their final place of work. You should depend on your job's life insurance policy only as a portion of the insurance you need. With outside coverage, many Gen Xers arbitrarily buy $250,000 or $500,000 of life insurance to "cover the mortgage." Anything less than $1,000,000 is likely too little insurance. For those with incomes over $100,000 a year, the life insurance number is closer to the several million range than a "flat" $1,000,000.

2. Make sure your term life insurance is convertible (for 10, 20, or 30 years).
Insurance companies generally play on a bingo board. What this means is that, depending on your age, health, and other factors,, there are particular companies that price their term insurance product to win that space. If you buy term insurance, your insurance agent should be able to show you rates for five or 10 different carriers. If you are buying the term insurance product from a proprietary agent, odds are you aren't getting the best deal and that is where they make their best commission. Most of the level term insurance policies do have a clause that allows you to convert these to a permanent policy without evidence of insurability. That's the key part to the equation. If your term insurance isn't convertible, you could run the risk of becoming uninsurable down the road if you develop a "pre-existing condition, but still needing insurance coverage.

3. Get some type of permanent policy.
People avoid buying permanent insurance because they think it costs too much, they don't understand it, or they read somewhere that it

doesn't make sense. Suze Orman says so, which must make it true. With permanent insurance there are various types of product structures, cost structures, and companies that are engaged in selling these products. You should do your homework to figure out which type makes the most sense for you, but what should be true for most of you in that early 40's range is that getting some type of permanent policy will ensure you have insurance coverage for life.

Most people don't go home at night or wake up in the morning thinking about how much life insurance they need. Most people think that nothing is ever going to happen to them, but it's never too early to start planning. Smart financial planning means not only looking at your overall financials, but assessing what types of coverages you will need at different ages and stages in life. Make sure to always consult an independent insurance agent who can represent many carriers or pay a fee-based insurance advisor to help guide you through this difficult maze of insurance decisions.

Top 5 Insurance Policies To Avoid

Doesn't it seem like there is always an insurance decision to make? Whether it is from a new purchase you make, a decision at work, or someone calling you to buy something over the phone, insurance decisions are being made every other month in our financial plans. It is often confusing to figure out which insurance programs make sense, and which are a waste of money. While hindsight is 20/20, here are five insurance policies you want to avoid.

1. Mortgage Insurance.

When you buy a new home, you will typically get a mailer to buy an insurance policy that will completely pay off the mortgage upon your death. If you are reasonably healthy, buying a level term insurance policy through any of the major insurance companies will often be much cheaper than buying this type of insurance.

2. Wedding Insurance.

Isn't there a bigger problem if you are buying insurance in the event your wedding doesn't happen? While the premiums on these policies may only range from $200 to $500, you need to really review exactly what the policy covers. Spend the money on doing something fun for your guests at the wedding. The risk trade-off isn't good enough on this one.

3. Credit Life Insurance.

This type of insurance will typically pay off your credit card at death. The premium will seem miniscule, usually costing less than $1 per month. However, if you are reasonably healthy, getting appropriate term or permanent life insurance that will cover credit card debt will be a better buy in the long run.

4. Air Travel Life Insurance.

You need a certain amount of life insurance –not more life insurance if you die on an airplane. If you want to go to Vegas to have some fun and bet, go ahead and book a room. You probably don't want to be betting on your own death with a double down on the next flight? Air travel is still the safest form of travel, and the least likely place for you to collect on this type of insurance.

5. Private Mortgage Insurance.

How do you avoid private mortgage insurance – or PMI? Make sure you put 20% down on a house. We know that is a novel idea, but maybe you just aren't ready to buy the type and size of house you are shopping for unless you can make the down payment. This insurance can be costly for a new homeowner.

It's not that the having insurance on to pay off credit card debt or your home at the time of your death isn't a good idea. It is. It is that there are often more cost-effective ways to get the same kind of coverage. Instead of buying these often frivolous and costly policies, you want to make sure you have adequate life insurance that will cover these expenses.

What Kind Of Term Insurance To Buy?

Many Gen Xers and Yers often wonder about what kind of term life insurance policy they should buy. Before you purchase life insurance, make sure to always have a discussion about your goals followed by an analysis so you can figure out the right amount of insurance you need. Then, you can focus on the right type of insurance. I've always viewed term life insurance like renting in an apartment. You are trying to provide your family with some level of protection/shelter for a period of time and then move out/eliminate the insurance. Here are three different ways you can look at buying the protection.

1. Group Term Insurance.

Many Gen Xers look to get their term life insurance coverage through work. For people in their 30s and early 40s, this can often be the most cost effective option in terms of price. Many employers will allow you to buy some multiple of your salary between 2 to 8 times your income depending on the plan. These are great because they are low cost. However, Gen Xers tend to change jobs often and the new company may not have the same type of coverage. What could be worse, however, is if your health changes over a period of a few years and you are unable to get outside coverage because you put all of your "life insurance eggs" with your group term insurance. This is a big mistake Gen Xers don't consider because they still feel young and healthy.

2. Low-cost non-convertible term insurance.

The best way to look at buying term insurance is to determine how long you will need the insurance and purchase a level premium/ amount of a level period of time. For example, if you have 20 years left on your mortgage and your kids are under the age of 10, a 20-year level term policy might make the most sense. It's best to run 10, 20, and 30-year term insurance numbers before you purchase policies so you can see the pricing across the board. One of the downside risks with most of these term insurance policies is that they are not convertible. You could keep the insurance forever at a higher premium in most cases, but cannot convert it to a permanent insurance policy should you have a need for more permanent protection.

3. Convertible term insurance.

One of the challenges in comparing term insurance premiums boils down to whether or not the policies are convertible. You could have two different 30-year level premium term insurance policies side-by-side with one being priced at $200 more per year than the other. The difference in price can often be explained in this way: For example, if your term insurance policy is $500,000, you can convert this policy to a permanent life insurance policy without evidence of insurability. This can be a big deal especially if over the course of 5 or 10 years your health changes.

For people marrying later in their 30's/early 40's and still having kids, it's best to look into insurance coverage before you turn 45 when rates can really jump up and your health will generally begin to deteriorate. Make sure to always consult an independent insurance agent who can represent many carriers or pay a fee-based insurance advisor to help guide you through this difficult maze of insurance decisions.

Why "Conditional Receipt" Is A Must When You Apply For Life Insurance

It's never fun having a discussion to figure out how much life insurance you need. Most people dread this conversation as much as going to buy a new car because you will always feel like the insurance agents are ready to pounce in order to make a sale. I have still yet to hear a surviving spouse tell me that they bought too much life insurance.

In many married couples, it is still usually one spouse who drives the conversation about how much life insurance the family needs – usually the major breadwinner of the family. Recently, I heard another sad story from a surviving spouse whose husband passed away way before his time. When I learned a little more about the situation, she revealed that he had been approved for a large sum of life insurance a few years back but didn't take it because he felt he could get a better rating. A couple of years later, he reapplied for life insurance and actually got a better rating. However, after being wishy washy over which policy to take when he was approved, he never made a decision to take any of the policies and left the family without any life insurance because he died. The face amount of insurance had actually been approved, but he just didn't accept and pay for the policy to put it in effect.

This is where the term "conditional receipt" becomes an important conversation that most families glance over when they apply for life insurance. When you take an insurance application, naturally there is going to be a period from the time you sign the application until the date the application actually gets approved. In between those dates, you'll have to do a phone interview, likely take a blood sample, ekg, and other healthcare screenings depending on the amount of insurance you apply for at that time. Typically, the insurance company will ask for certain records from all of your physicians so they can do the best job possible in ascertaining what rating you should get for the life insurance.

You have the option at the time of the application to submit a first month's premium or submit no premium at all. The important part to attaching an initial premium called "conditional receipt" is that if the policy gets approved (it must get approved and not just be in underwriting) and you die prior to the policy being delivered, it will still be considered binding by the insurance company because you submitted the premium for the first month (or year) along with the application. Remember to check the exact meaning of "conditional receipt" with each insurance company when you apply for life insurance. Imagine that the policy is approved and waiting delivery as referenced in the case above. The family would still qualify to get the death benefit simply by attaching the first month's premium to the policy. You are only risking the opportunity cost of earning a few pennies of interest in the bank while your money is deposited with the insurance company during the underwriting process.

Much like insurance at a Black Jack table in Las Vegas, many people simply forgo paying this amount with the application because they see it being a waste of money floating their cash with an insurance company for a few months. However, I recommend that you always submit an initial amount with the policy if you are serious about the insurance because you never know what unforeseen circumstances could arise between application and delivery. This small amount could make a huge difference for your family should something prematurely happen to you, so consider doing a "conditional receipt" the next time you apply for life insurance.

22 Questions to Ask About Disability Insurance

There are many types of insurance programs to manage these days. Yet, one type of insurance most misunderstood by employees of companies and small business owners is the need for disability insurance to protect income. Since there are so many nuances of disability insurance, here are some key questions to ask yourself regarding your personal situation.

1. What percentage of income will be replaced?

Most employer programs cover between 50% and 66% of income if you become disabled. That means that some other kind of insurance will need to cover between 34% and 50 % of your regular income.

2. Will commissions and/or bonuses be covered?

In most cases, your employer will only cover your base salary. If you have a large bonus program or work commissions, you need to really review the fine print of your group policy.

3. Does disability insurance cover 401(k) and other retirement contributions?

Generally, this is not covered. The big question then is how will you continue to fund your retirement goals?

4. Can the payout increase with future income?

For a small amount of money, you can attach a rider that will allow you to increase the amount of disability insurance coverage you have without having to prove evidence of insurability.

5. Is the payout adjusted for cost of living?

If you begin collecting a disability insurance claim, you want to make sure you have the rider to increase your payout benefit by inflation every year.

6. Is there a maximum payout per year?

You want to make sure you aren't capped by the policy on how much you can get paid out every year.

7. Is the payout taxable?

If your employer pays for the coverage, then it will be taxable income to you. If you pay for the premium, then it will be tax free to you when you receive benefits.

8. If I can't return to the job I had before, or can't work at all, what happens to the payouts?

The key to this part of the policy is that if you cannot do the duties of your own occupation that the policy will still pay you even if you can be a hot dog vendor at the ballpark.

10. Will the policy renew annually at the same price?

It is truly important to have a program that is guaranteed renewable and non cancellable.

11. Are there any circumstances under which the policy can be cancelled?

The policy should always be non-cancellable as long as you pay the premiums.

13. Is there a waiting period?

The big question here is that you need to have an adequate cash reserve if your company program does not have a good short-term disability program. One key decision that affects price is how long your waiting period will be on the policy. If you have a larger cash reserve and can sustain a disability for six months or a year, the longer you make the waiting period, the smaller your premium will be every year.

16. How does working at home function with the unhazardous workplace requirement?

17. How does being self-employed affect my ability to get a policy?
Generally the insurance company will want to see two years of tax returns if you are self employed and will only look at your net income in the business for coverage.

18. What injuries or illnesses do policies typically exclude?
If you've already been treated for depression or back pain or cancer will you not cover those maladies at all in the future? If you have had chronic back pain in the past, for example, the company may issue a policy but put an exclusion in it for that specific injury.

20. Is it possible to erase some of these exclusions a few years after my policy goes into effect if I don't come down with those afflictions during that period?

21. How do policies work with federal Social Security disability benefits?
You need to make sure when you purchase coverage that you get base coverage and not coverage that integrates with social security. If your coverage integrates with social security and you begin collecting social security, your amount paid to you from the insurance will reduce if it is not the base coverage.

22. Can the policy be transferred to a new job?
Most people think a disability means that you are unable to work at all. With new disabilities such as depression and carpel tunnel syndrome, you really need to review whether your policy covers your own occupation or any occupation as this can be important with respect to how much you may be able to collect. If you have never

reviewed this, now may be a good time to do this so you can make sure that your financial house is adequately protected.

Snoop Dogg Gets Approved Preferred Rates For Life Insurance?

As insurance rules and regulations get more complicated, it really pays to have an insurance agent who knows what they are doing on your side. The truth is we don't have the foggiest idea if Snoop Dogg got approved preferred rates for life insurance, but what we do know is that it has been alleged that Snoop Dogg, Lady GaGa, and Willie Nelson have all rolled a joint or two in their lives. As of May 2015, 23 states, plus Washington, DC., have legalized medical marijuana and four of these states have also legalized possession of pot. Are there important things for you to know about this when you apply for life insurance?

Of course having written insurance policies for over 20 years, I've heard just about everything when I take an application. "Uhhh...will marijuana show up on blood test?" "If I've smoked pot, how long do you figure it will take for it to flush out of my system?" That's funny. Too funny. What are we? A part-time doctor that has accuracy testing for flushing drugs out of your system? You should have thought of that way before you toked up on that 'j' before the Jay-Z concert. Or, just maybe, if you know the rules about what insurance companies are actually looking at/for, it wouldn't really matter at all.

What really becomes most important is the cover letter your insurance agent writes with the application. Remember, insurance underwriting has subjectivity within the process. For example, when it comes to cigars, many insurance carriers will allow for a celebratory cigar or two and still treat you as a non-smoker when it comes to underwriting. Insurance carriers like Met Life and Mutual of Omaha may actually look at you as a non-smoker with recreational use of marijuana. Knowing what carriers to go to and how to write your application are crucial. Remember, if you falsify your application, you could be under a permanent window where a claim can be denied because you misrepresented material facts of your insurance case.

Since pretty much everyone denies that they have tried or smoked pot, we're not here to be your conscious. Even the last three Presidents openly admit that they tried pot at one time or another. Although according to him, Clinton didn't inhale. Depending on the use of marijuana, the state you live in, and your overall insurance application, you too may be able to get approved, preferred rates. Don't let your insurance case go up in smoke. Get with an agent who can help you with the finer points of this process and you can make a smart money move saving hundreds or thousands of dollars on your bottom line!

Five Insurance Policies Every Small Business Owner Needs

This is the weekend you have finally decided it's time to start your own business. You've had enough of the corporate rat race and now you want to take matters into your own hands. After you determine whether you want to set up as a sole proprietor, LLC, S-Corporation, or C-Corporation, there will be a litany of items to strike off the checklist to ensure the business is up and running. One of the key areas most small business owners ignore is getting the right insurance policies as they initiate their new businesses. Even as the business gets established, business owners often ignore getting the right type of protection in place to insulate their business in case of unforeseen circumstances. Here are five insurance policies every small business owner needs.

1. Disability Insurance.

The challenge most new business owners don't understand is that if you show no verifiable income, you'll have no chance of getting disability insurance. This type of insurance is designed to protect your personal income in the event that you can't do the duties of your own occupation. Make sure the disability insurance you purchase covers your "own occupation" vs. "any occupation." In addition, ensure that you have a cost of living adjustment and a future purchase option to buy more insurance if your income goes up.

2. Health Insurance.

If you are leaving your corporate job, one of the main considerations is whether to continue with COBRA from your former employer or buy an individual policy through the new federal exchange. Is the best idea to get a Health Savings Account attached to a high deductible health plan, a catastrophic insurance policy, or go for the PPO option with a lower overall family deductible? What will the cost of COBRA be for your family now that you are paying 100% of the premium? Do you need the exact coverage you had while working for an employer? How long does the coverage last? Could you get a better deal on the Federal health insurance exchange?

3. Business Owner's Policy.

This type of policy is usually bundled in packs that would cover several different areas for a business owner. Many of these policies cover items such as property insurance, basic liability insurance, some vehicle coverage insurance, business interruption insurance, bodily injury insurance, and renter's coverage insurance.

4. E & O Insurance or Professional Liability Insurance.

This can be tricky, but generally these types of policies can give your business some protection for either improperly rendering services or protecting against lawsuits/complaints depending on the type of industry where your business resides. Although these policies are traditionally designed for professions such as lawyers, accountants, and doctors, you should determine if you have exposure in your business to protect.

5. Life Insurance (Buy-Sell Insurance).

Often, most people who make a transition into a business leave the bulk of their life insurance behind at their employer. Getting your life insurance policies in place before you leave your employer is a good idea. If you have a business partner, one important thing to get squared away is setting up a buy-sell agreement to make sure that cash is in place to protect your families and the business.

There are another half dozen different types of insurance policies you will want to consider when you begin to grow your new business. Since cash flow may be tight, many new owners forego paying for these insurances to save money. However, growing your business while walking on a high wire is not the best advice. Get the right types of insurance policies in place and you will be able to focus on growing top line revenue without worrying about a ticking time bomb at your door.

Four Lessons We Can Learn From Tony Soprano's Estate

"You woke up this morning and got yourself a gun, Mama always said you'd be the chosen one." Am I the only one who sorely misses The Sopranos on HBO on Sunday night? No matter what happened during the weekend, I could always count on a gripping hour of drama, and seeing the slicked back hair of Paulie Walnuts. With the passing of TV and movie superstar James Gandolfini, he will be sadly missed for some of his great work as Tony Soprano. At times like this, there are always lessons to be learned. Gandolfini did a few smart things with his estate, but he also made some major mistakes that you can learn from.

1. Not making use of the unlimited marital deduction.

Gandolfini left his $70 million estate to his two sisters, his wife, and his daughter. His son was the beneficiary of a life insurance policy not included in his estate. Although the optimal estate planning wouldn't be to outright leave everything to your spouse because he or she could face estate taxes when he or she passes away. By not using the unlimited marital deduction, it could cost Gandolfini's estate upwards of $30 million dollars in estate taxes. Even though his current wife was the natural born mother of his son, there are smarter strategies he could have deployed including setting up bypass trusts, using irrevocable insurance trusts, charitable remainder trusts, and a host of other trust strategies.

2. Update your will often.

Gandolfini's most recent update of his last will and testament was on December 19, 2012. The will was updated after the birth of his daughter Liliana. This allowed Mr. Gandolfini to make sure that Liliana was included in the estate as his only other child prior to this update was his son Michael. Without having made this important update, it's quite possible that Liliana would have been left out of the estate.

3. Incorrectly funding your trusts.

Gandolfini had actually set up an irrevocable life insurance trust, which is generally a trust that will buy an insurance policy to provide beneficiaries and heirs with instant liquidity to pay estate taxes down the road. These policies are not subject to income and and estate taxes because of the nature of the trust. The wise thing Gandolfini did was fund the trust with a $7 million policy. However, his overall estate tax is going to be a lot higher than that number. Had he updated the policies and the amounts, the tax could have been paid by life insurance proceeds and the beneficiaries would have been able to retain the wealth he worked hard to build over his career.

4. Have co-trustees.

When you are dealing with minor children, you need to make sure you update your custodian designation. If you manage to build wealth over your lifetime, you may need to set up trusts for your kids that will take effect at death through your will. It's important when you have different parties involved (several kids from different marriages, multiple spouses, and family members) to appoint more than one trustee for your estate. In Gandolfini's estate, he appointed his current wife, his sister, and a third party. This gives an excellent check and balance system for oversight of the funds.

Planning an estate can result in some difficult choices and tough conversations. Every time we see a public figure like this make mistakes, there are a least a dozen other stories we hear from the average families who just didn't understand the rules before it was too late. Perhaps it's time for you to have a family-style Soprano dinner sometime soon to figure out what type of estate plan makes sense for you and your family.

Ten Things To Include In Your Will

1. Name a personal representative or executor.

In an individual will, you can name a person or institution to act as a personal representative, called an executor in some states, who will be responsible for making sure that the will is carried out as written and that the property is divvied up and distributed as directed. It's also wise to name an alternate in case the first choice is unable or unwilling to act.

2. Name beneficiaries to get specific property.

Your will can specify separate gifts of property - called specific bequests - including cash, personal property, or real estate. Likely beneficiaries for such bequests are children and other relatives, but they may also include friends, business associates, charities, or other organizations.

3. Specify alternate beneficiaries.

In fashioning their wills, most people assume that the beneficiaries they name will survive to take the property they've specified for them. The most thoughtful wills provide for what should happen if those beneficiaries don't survive - either by naming a backup recipient or indicating that the person's spouse or children should take the property instead.4. Name someone to take all remaining property - If you have opted to make specific bequests of property, a will is also the place to name people or organizations to take whatever property is left over. This property is usually called a "residuary estate."

5. Give directions on dividing personal assets.

If you want assets divided among children, charities, or other beneficiaries, the will should note precisely what property is included in that pool. It should also specify whether assets are to go directly to beneficiaries or whether they're to be sold and the value divided among the beneficiaries, either equally or according to stated percentages.

6. Give directions for allocating business assets.

Business assets are often separate from personal assets - and most business owners have specific ideas about what should be done with them after their deaths. If you are a business owner and don't have a written plan covering the windup of your business, see an experienced estate planning attorney to ensure that your wishes are clearly indicated in your will.

7. Specify how debts, expenses, and taxes should be paid.
The will should spell out your wishes regarding how to settle debts and final expenses, such as funeral and probate costs, as well as any estate and inheritance taxes. Usually a specific source, such as a bank account, will be tagged to cover these costs.

8. Cancel debts others owe.
A nice added touch is that people making wills can use the documents to relieve those who owed them money from the responsibility of paying that debt, along with any accrued interest, to their survivors.

9. Indicate special instructions for maintaining real estate.
If you name someone to keep your house (or houses), you should list specific instructions for its care and upkeep in your will.

10. Provide a caretaker for pets.
Since the law considers pets to be property, the best way for to ensure a good home for your pet is to leave the animal to someone named in your will who has agreed to give it a good home. Many people also leave that person an amount of money to help cover caretaking expenses.

5 Important Financial Questions To Ask Your Parents

Talking about money is never an easy subject. It can be particularly difficult to talk about money and estate planning with your parents. As you watch your parents get into their 60s, 70s, or 80s, there are some key questions that you will want to talk about to ensure their finances are in good shape. Good or bad, you will have to deal with these issues down the road.

1. Do your parents have a will/living trust?

If they don't have a written one, then the state they live in will have one for them. My guess is that you don't want the state to decide how your parent's assets should be distributed. The will has many features, but most importantly it allows your parent's to say which personal items go to which children along with an orderly administration of the estate. Depending on the size of the estate and other factors, your parents may need one or multiple trusts.

2. Do your parents have a durable power of attorney?

In my mind, the durable power of attorney is one of the most important legal documents for older parents to have as part of their estate plan. Along with a medical durable power of attorney, someone is going to have to be responsible for making financial and medical decisions should your parents become incapable of making those decisions themselves. Without the durable power of attorney, you will have to go to court to get appointed as your parent's guardian. Having seen thousands of financial planning cases, this will be the very last thing you want to do a time of crisis.

3. Have your parents investigated long-term care insurance?

In recent years more and more people are being sent to nursing homes after being diagnosed with Alzheimer's disease. These types of situations are often emotionally traumatic, but most don't realize the financial devastation to the estate. Most people don't choose Medicare as much as it chooses them. Your parents can easily blow through a few hundred thousand dollars in a short period of time with the rising cost of full time care. It makes a ton of sense to encourage them to look at long term care insurance while they can still qualify for it.

4. Have your parents recently checked titling of assets and beneficiary designations?

With today's world of marriages, divorces, and remarriages, it is important that your parents review their beneficiary designations on financial documents such as insurance policies and IRA accounts. They should review both primary and contingent beneficiaries every year to be certain that those assets are directed exactly where they want them to go. It is also a good idea to have discussions about whether you should be joined with them on items such as a bank account, real estate property, or other investment assets.

5. What happens if... and where is everything?

One of the biggest estate planning mistakes is just simply that the kids don't know where everything is that their parents own. This doesn't mean your mom or dad has to tell you every account balance or all of the details of their will, but simply where the documents are should something unforeseen happen to them. We have our clients use an online storage vault and screen scraping on line personal financial dashboard to make this process more efficient. If your parents are travelling in their retirement years this information will be important to know.

I like to have family planning meetings as sometimes I can help facilitate these discussions. As you get together with your parents over the next year, spend some time asking these important questions. It may make all the difference in preserving your family wealth.

Chapter 10

How To Make Work Optional

Retirement: The Holy Grail. It's the destination many of us have been working toward our whole lives. But what will your retirement actually look like? In this chapter, we're going to discuss some strategies to begin realistically thinking about to create the retirement you want. Some of this will be tough – once you land on your "number," you have to do the work to get there. There is nothing worse than deciding to retire, spending a year or two in retirement only to have to go back to work because you did not plan properly. I don't want that to happen to you. So, let's talk about getting to your realistic number.

I Just Want To Be In Charge Of Me

Most college graduates dream of landing a job with a Fortune 500 company. Most of us want to get a good company on our resume so we can begin building our careers. For many, the thought of working your way up the ladder is truly exciting, and when you meet your first "big boss" with the cushy corner office, it gets you motivated to work harder for your dreams. Many of these big companies flashed fancy trips, stock options, and powerful titles at you. In return, you follow the bouncing ball and drink whatever Kool-Aid the powers were serving for breakfast, lunch, and dinner.

So what's this movement we are beginning to see here in the United States? Is it the loner movement? Is it a trend line of more people who want to work in their pajamas at home? Is this a monumental shift in the course of time that your friend isn't your cube mate next door but rather the noise coming from your computer? What's happened to all of those hard charging bulls that wanted to become Senior Vice President and rule the world someday?

I'm not sure at what point it happens in someone's career, but it happens quicker today than in previous generations. It's not exactly burnout - because walking away from a $250,000 a year job isn't all that easy to do, especially when it comes with bonuses and other perks. It's more a point of utter saturation with babysitting whining employees, incessantly dealing with your HR department, and shaking hands with faces of people whose name you cannot remember. Wow! "I just can't wait for next year's national conference to hang out with our 2,000 closest friends," you say that to yourself on the flight out only to count down the hours until you get back home.

For more client meetings than I can remember, I hear this familiar refrain from friends and clients alike. Many are searching for the passion to wake up for work every morning, get out of bed, and be in charge of themselves. No employees. No headaches. No reporting. No mid-year reviews. No unplanned sales conferences. Just the ability to take care of you and your destiny. The trend is that many people would rather have a consulting job making $100,000 a year than dealing with all of the B.S. of Corporate America in order to make a few bucks more… if they could figure out a way to do it.

So I offer this up to you. We will see a quantum shift in the ways people handle their financial planning over the next 10 years. We call this exit planning. How can we exit what we don't enjoy doing today and maximize our financial resources to build a bridge so we can get to the other side of what we would love to be doing every day.

Taking charge of you, once and for all, won't be easy, but with a little bit of planning and forethought, it may just be you, your computer, and morning television for next year's daily roll call. As Al Pacino would say "Hoo-hah!" That's the scent of being in charge of me right down the hallway.

Is It Too Late To Begin Saving For Retirement?

You are 45 years old and it dawns on you that your college days are getting further and further away in your review view mirror and you can see the exit sign for retirement inching closer. As you sit down at your kitchen table to really assess your overall financial situation, you begin to ponder the life and financial mistakes you have made. You wonder to yourself, "Should I even bother trying to save? Is it too late for me to begin saving for retirement?"

I've seen many people come to my office at this juncture in life. Typically there is a personal story about how their financial picture would be better if it wasn't for the bad real estate decision, the mid-life divorce, or a failed business venture. When retirement is beginning to stare you in the face, it's not easy to admit you may be behind. If you have $10,000 in your savings account and $50,000 in 401(k)/retirement assets, it may seem insurmountable to reach the mountain of one day making work optional. So when is it too late to begin saving for retirement?

The short answer to this is never. You should never feel like you are so far behind that you shouldn't begin setting goals to achieve your dream of making work optional. Here are the steps you should take to get yourself on the right track.

1. Set goals.

The most important thing at the start of the process is to set some defined goals. So maybe at this point in life you aren't going to have 5 million dollars in retirement, but the key is finding out how much you would need in addition to social security and other pensions to be able to save now to help you recreate a paycheck down the road. You can also figure out how conservative or aggressive you'll need to be with your investing plan based upon the financial plan you put in place. Most importantly, once you create goals, review them on a regular basis to make sure you are on the right track and if you need to make adjustments.

2. Get your expenses in order.

Remember, at age 45, the next 15 to 20 years should be your peak earning years. If you get your fixed and discretionary expenses in order, you'll be able to save more of those bonuses and salary increases as they happen. One of the keys to make up the ground you lost from early compounding of your retirement assets is to minimize your expenses. This means take on a smaller house, buy used cars, and don't expand your lifestyle if your income increases.

3. Pay down debt.

As your approach the retirement exit, you want to be sure you pay down all consumer debt. You will also want to work aggressively on trying to pay down your mortgage. If you can't save up enough money then reducing overall expenses will be an important part of this equation.

4. Take advantage of catch-up rules.

Turning 50 is usually a big birthday milestone. While you may take a dream vacation or throw a rock star-like party on this day, it actually triggers an important switch when it comes to savings. For both your

401(k) plan at work and for your IRA/Roth IRA contributions, you can actually start to put away more money into these plans. Once you turn fifty, if you have the cash flow, you should immediately accelerate to the maximum on all of these catch up provisions.

5. Talk to your kids.
If one of the reasons you are in this bind is because your children are living the good life at your expense, it is probably time to sit down and have a straight talk about why things need to change. While we all want our kids to have a better life than we did, making financial decisions like over the top birthday parties, expensive vacations, and holiday times that even Santa Clause couldn't afford is just a poor money move. Ask a 21 year-old if they remember all of the gifts they got from the ages of 5 to 10 years-old, and they just won't be able to tell you.

One of the greatest comedians of all time is Rodney Dangerfield. He's just one of those guys who can make you laugh before he's even said the punch line. He started in his comedy career in his early 40's and became a huge success late in life. Although his favorite line was "I don't get no respect!" it is never too late for you to get some financial respect to achieve your dreams. It won't be "easy money" and you might have to go "back to school," but you can still save enough to help make work optional down the road.

How A Threesome Can Improve Your Retirement
I'm officially thinking that most men (and many women too) who read this headline are thinking, "Have you officially lost your mind trying to connect the words threesome and retirement?" The answer is no, I haven't lost my mind. For the record, I'm not going to suggest you run out and have a threesome, although you've probably fantasized about it once in your lifetime. So how can a threesome actually improvement your retirement?

The ménage-a-trois I am talking about are the three players you need to fall in love with to be able to retire successfully. Within the X and Y Generation, the philosophies that have been espoused in many of the major publications will likely fail because they only talk about statistics and numbers. What most common retirement strategies fail to mention is the psychology behind the strategy and how it affects the person who is trying to make work optional. Here are the three strategies to look for under the cover if you want to understand the threesome strategy.

1. You must have a pension.
People who retire with large 401(k) balances, sell a business for a pile of cash, or build up massive sums of money in the bank actually have a problem that they didn't realize they would have when they were building up their money. It's the psychology of "I'm not going to go broke" that actually becomes a detriment to the way people behave when they retire. This attitude is actually a deterrent from allowing people to enjoy retirement because anytime you see the account value of your bank account or brokerage statement go down, you immediately revert back to a mentality that you can't do anything, or you might run out of money. I've seen this with many retirees who have constant panic and stress as they watch the daily values of their accounts fluctuate. Even if you don't have a pension at work, setting up a program with an insurance company to provide you with some sort of guaranteed monthly income when you retire is actually a good thing because each month you will get a check directly deposited in your account. Find anyone you know that had an old traditional company pension and ask them how happy they are that they don't have to worry about the bond or stock market every day.

2. You must have a paid off house.
I recently learned an interesting thing: by purchasing a smaller house

and aggressively paying off the mortgage, people were given the financial freedom to use a smaller capital base and other passive streams of income to technically have made work optional. Either way, you must fall in love with the strategy of paying off your house. When I started in the financial services industry, I was always told by managers that people could do better off in the stock market than they could on their house, especially if interest rates were low. Forget about the financial analysis to determine which is better, and focus here on the powerful emotional feeling you have knowing that you owe NOBODY! In my opinion, it will be one of the best decisions that you will ever make.

3. You must fall in love with work that keeps you alive.
Recently, a friend of mine had a car service take him home from the airport. During the car ride, he mentioned that he had one of the most wonderful conversations with a 77 year-old driver who remind-ed him of Alfred from Batman. The driver actually had a cooler of beers waiting for him in the car, Nutrigrain bars, and several choices of fruit. The driver proceeded to tell him about how he has been in and around the car business for the last 60 years. He told my friend that he actually drove race cars competitively and he still drives cars today as this is his life's passion. He never plans to "retire," but is truly enjoying his retirement staying active with work he loves to do. Why do you have to wait to come alive in retirement if you are dead every day going to work? Seems like that would be backwards. When you love what you do, there will always be a way to make an income stream.

From the title of this section, I bet some of you had a flashback to Jack Tripper from Three's Company. If you have daydreamed about having a threesome, perhaps this financial threesome can give you the retirement fantasy you have also dreamed about. The ability to do what you want to do, when you want to do it, without having to really think about money. That's a smart money move for retirement.

What Are Your Retirement Assumptions

You often see commercials asking the question, "What's Your Number"? What they are really referring to is the notion of how much money you think you need in order to be able to retire. It's funny that most people we talk to today don't really call it retirement. They really think about the term of making work optional. This means having the ability to do what they want when they want irrespective of money.

We have always thought about our "work optional" number being the amount of money we actually need on a debit card when we retire to maintain our standard of living the way we want it when we go "work optional." The mistake that we see in many financial plans is that the assumptions made by the clients or their financial advisors are too aggressive. Making a set of aggressive assumptions can often make it appear that you will be able to retire comfortably, when in reality the sum of all of those assumptions may leave you grossly underfunded. So, how can your assumptions make your retirement planning fail?

1. Inflation.

Most financial plans I see have the ability to make an assumption on inflation. Over the 50-year period from 1956 to 2006, inflation ran at a rate of 4.09%, and over the 20-year period from 1986 to 2006 inflation ran at a rate of 3.09%. The majority of financial planners use a whole number of 3% for inflation because it has been low as of late. Using a 3% vs. a 4% for inflation assumption can mean literally hundreds of thousands of dollars difference in your retirement planning projections. The conservative assumption to use would be 4%.

If you are using 3%, this may leave you with a tremendous shortfall in retirement if we go through a higher inflationary period over the next 50 years.

2. Tax rate.

There are typically two types of tax rates: marginal rate and effective rate. The marginal tax rate is the tax rate on the very last dollar of income that comes into your household. The effective rate is you overall tax rate on your money. Most financial plans show a 20% tax rate. You want to make sure your assumptions take into consideration your overall effective tax rate, state tax rate, and local/city tax rate, if applicable. Often, people assume they will have a lower tax rate when they retire because they will make less money. However, tax rates may be higher or lower when you retire irrespective of how much money you make. In addition, do you really plan to have a lot less income when you retire?

3. Rate of return.

Financial plans often have to assume a rate of return on your money from now until you retire, and what return you will earn after you retire. First, you want to ensure all returns are considering what will happen on an after-tax basis. Second, be certain you aren't using double-digit returns on your pre-retirement rate of return, as that will likely be too aggressive. Third, you need to be sure you move the post-retirement return to be a couple of percentage points below where your pre-retirement as you will likely dial down your risk. You should be 100% certain the plan you put in place really matches your risk tolerance.

4. Asset Growth Before and After Retirement.

This is a really important one. What rate of return did your financial advisor use for your asset growth of 401(k)'s, investment accounts, etc. Did they use 0%, 4%, 7%, or 10% or more? Every 1% better rate of return substantially shrinks the asset pool you will need at retirement. What happens if the markets return exactly what they did the last 15 years? Most people focus on the assumption only up to retirement age, but your financial advisor also has to project returns after retirement. Did they use the same exact number after you retire that was used before you retire? If you did, your plan is a disaster as most people reduce their risk after retirement. Far too often, financial advisors will show you your retirement picture, but not discuss which assets they said would be available for retirement. Did you add the rental properties, which may or may not have equity? Were some of these accounts earmarked for a different purpose? Be sure you know what assets will be used solely for retirement.

5. Social Security.

Do you believe Social Security will be here at the level it is today? Most financial planners assume you will earn maximum Social Security and start taking it at age 62. A conservative financial plan will assume you don't get Social Security. The more aggressive plans will assume you get the full boat of Social Security benefits.

6. Savings and additional resources.

The last piece of being realistic about what financial resources you can commit (lump sum or monthly savings) to your retirement goals. Some financial plans show savings increasing by 3 or 4% per year. If you build this assumption into your plan, your retirement numbers will look easier to achieve. However, you need to make sure you and your financial planner follow through on increasing those savings practically every year. On-going savings rate is also one of the most important calculations in your retirement plan. How much did your financial advisor say you will need to save every year until retirement? Did he or she show your company continuing to match your

401(k) plan? Did they show you getting stock options every year? Best in my mind to show nothing so you can really see what will need to be saved.

7. Your Home.

Did you include or exclude your home equity as potential retirement income. If you showed selling your home in retirement, what rate of return did your advisor use on real estate? Was it 5%, 7%, 10%?

8. Life Expectancy.

Hardly ever, do financial advisors have this discussion. When you run retirement projections, showing the difference of dying at the age of 85 or the age of 90 can add or subtract a $500,000 to $1 million dollar difference in the nest egg you will need in retirement.

9. Living Expenses.

What number did you use for living expenses? Was this a gross number or a net number of taxes? This is an important question to ask. Did you show expenses increasing with inflation or not? Did you show what will happen with expenses if one or the other spouse has a need for long term care?

A retirement plan isn't an exercise that can be done once and then reviewed every 5 to 10 years. In fact, the day you put your plan together it will likely change dramatically a year later due to stock market rates of return, tax law changes, and/or changes in your personal situation. Having a set of conservative assumptions in your plan will give you more margin for error over time. If your assumptions are too aggressive, you may feel like you are on track and then fall woefully short of your goals.

Pay Off Credit Cards Or Save For Retirement?

You just turned 30, and still have credit card debt hanging over your head. While you were out partying and paying off student loans during your 20s, you realize that you haven't saved a nickel for retirement. The debate begins in your head. Do you pay off the $10,000 of credit card debt or do you save the maximum you can in your 401(k)?

The Dave Ramsey's of the world would always say to pay off debt first before saving for retirement. I don't agree with this one-size-fits-all approach because it really does depend on your personal situation.

The first variable is whether or not your company offers a matching 401(k) plan. For example, if you put away 6% of your salary and your company matches 3% it would be an instant 50% return on your money if you stay with your company long enough to earn the match. Some companies may also offer a discounted stock purchase plan that would give you a discount on its stock. Especially with the 401(k), the match, and the time value of money getting started on a matching 401(k) plan, is likely to be a good idea if you are 30 years old.

When you consider your overall debt, it is important to pay off all of your non-deductible debt, such as credit card loans, as some debt, such as your home mortgage, will have tax advantages for you. Some of these loans may be consolidated into a low interest rate or temporary zero interest rate, which could help you keep your overall balances lower. I am a big fans of paying off your lowest dollar balance card first versus the highest interest rate card because I believe seeing a victory only leads to more victories.

Doing a thorough analysis is an important step in choosing retirement savings vs. debt, but I recommend doing both versus one or the other and here is why: Being financially successful is as much emotional as it is financial. Smaller wins in your money get you to believe you can have bigger wins—it makes you smart emotionally. You work hard to pay off your debt, but if you see nothing in retirement you may feel defeated. The same is true if you save a lot for retirement, but never pay down your debt. Setting realistic goals and growing your assets while reducing your debt will help you feel emotionally good about achieving the ultimate goal of being debt free and having financial independence. Don't let the math fool you because crunching numbers isn't the only financial analysis you should do.

Types Of Retirement Investment Vehicles

Once you figure out your number, there are really two very important ships that will get to that number. First, how much money do you need to save on a monthly basis to get to your number? Second, what rate of return on an after-tax basis do your assets need to earn to reach the retirement number? Let's review some of the vehicles you can use to work toward your retirement goal.

1. Employer sponsored retirement plan.

Most employers, whether they be companies, schools, hospitals, or government agencies, will have a retirement plan they sponsor that allows you to save for retirement. The 401(k) plan is probably the most widely known of all of these plans. 401(k) plans allow employees to put away pre-tax dollars into an account that will grow tax-deferred for their retirement. Some employers will offer a matching program for employee contributions, and if you stay with your company for 5 or 6 years you will generally vest in the free contributions made by your employer. You will have a series of investment choices where you can invest it yourself or the investment company will have a pre-designed investment portfolio for you based upon your target retirement age or date. If you are under 50 years-old, you can put away up to $16,000 per year, and when you are over 50, you can put away up to $22,000 each year in the plan. For those just beginning, most plans will allow you to contribute as little as 1% of your gross income.

A new feature catching on in 401(k) plans is an option for a Roth 401(k) plan within the overall employer sponsored retirement plan. This feature allows you to put away dollars on an after-tax basis irrespective of your family's gross income. You can still grow the money tax-deferred, but they will come out tax-free when you withdraw them out in retirement. With today's ever-changing tax environment, you should really consider strongly how you balance both pre-tax 401(k) and Roth 401(k) contributions.

2. IRA and Roth IRA plans.
If you have no employer-sponsored retirement plan, another option you have is to set up your own individual retirement account (IRA) or Roth individual retirement (Roth IRA) account. For those under 50, you can generally put away up to $5,000. For those over the age of 50, you can generally put away up to $6,000. The traditional IRA contributions can be deductible if you do not have an employer-sponsored retirement plan. If you do have a 401(k) plan, the contributions may or may not be deductible depending on your adjusted gross income. If you want to contribute to a Roth IRA, your annual adjusted gross income will determine whether you can make yearly Roth contributions. The key with both the IRA and Roth IRA plans is the power of tax-deferral until you need the funds during retirement. Many people try to contribute to a Roth IRA, as those contributions will be distributed tax-free during their retirement years.

3. Real estate.

Although many people saw the real estate bubble burst, real estate can be another investment vehicle to help prepare for retirement. This can be true for both residential and commercial real estate. Beyond the hope that real estate appreciates in value, some investors hope to rent their properties before retirement. This allows the real estate to provide an additional income stream in retirement if it continues to be rented. It is important to consider your experience in buying real estate as well as the decision to be a landlord should you choose to use this vehicle for retirement preparation.

4. Stock options, restricted stock, deferred compensation plans, and other work-sponsored programs.

The key here for most of you in these programs is to have a defined exit strategy out of these plans. Without setting a pre-determined exit price or stock option triggering strategy, you are not likely to be able to retire off the options management says will make you wealthy. In fact, many people spend the net cash earned from these options on buying a bigger primary residence, nice(r) cars, or swanky vacation homes. It takes serious consideration in these types of vehicles to really "earmark" what is actually going to be used for retirement.

5. Sale of your business.

I see many business owners who put all of their retirement eggs into the basket of selling their business. It is truly important to set up multiple strategies for your retirement vehicles, and not to bank solely on the sale of your business – even for the best business owners. Since there can be regulatory change, industry change, or employee change, in any business, a business can go from being worth a lot of money to a little in a short period of time. Think about the tech and real estate busts in the last 11 years that caused many businesses to be worth nothing almost overnight.

6. Cash-value life insurance.

One other option for those who max out their 401(k) and IRA/Roth IRA savings is overfunding a cash-value life insurance policy. If these policies are funded and managed appropriately, it is possible to use them to grow after tax assets tax deferred and withdraw those assets on a tax-free basis down the road. It is important to understand that cash value must be managed correctly in order to work properly as a retirement savings vehicle.

These vehicles are not an exhaustive list, but they will easily give you a great place to start when thinking about your retirement. No matter what vehicle(s) you use to fund your retirement, you will still need to figure out how much to save on a monthly basis and what rate of return your assets will need to earn to hit your "number."

Investing Within Your 401(k) and IRA's

Sometimes we think of retirement planning vehicles like a coffee cup. Each coffee cup is different in that it may or may not have sugar or cream (and how much of each) and any other list of variables that make a cup of coffee "good" to you. Similarly, retirement planning vehicles have different sets of rules and regulations that structure it. A coffee cup doesn't have to be used to drink coffee. You can put water, juice, soda, coffee, and much more in the coffee up. IRA's work the same way. The IRA is the coffee cup, and you can literally put almost any investment you want into it.

Before we start talking about the particulars of IRA investing strategies, let's review 401(k) plans. Most 401(k)'s will offer you three types of options. There are two important rules you should try to follow in your 401(k). First, act your age. What I mean here is the amount of fixed or bond-type investments should be around your current age. So, if you're 40, you should have 40% of your investments in fixed or bond-type investments. The remaining number should be in the equity side of your portfolio. Second, be sure you have checked the automatic rebalancing feature (quarterly) should your 401(k) provider offer this option. Here are your main three choices in the 401(k):

1. Lifecycle or target fund investments.
These investments are structured to give you a particular set of years when you think you are going to "retire," and get your investments set up where the investment company thinks a person with that time horizon should be properly allocated. Although I am not a big fan of investing your 401(k) this way, it is the easiest option to just put your 401(k) on auto-pilot.

2. Build your own portfolio.
Most 401(k) plans will have somewhere between 10 to 50 options depending on how your employer sets up the plan. Usually the larger the employer, the fewer choices you will have in the plan. The plan will give you historical data on how each mutual fund (or ETF) has performed in the plan. The important part for you to research is the manager running the fund. Sometimes a fund can have a great track record, but has recently changed management teams. The same can be true with a fund that performed poorly in the past. If a really good manager takes that fund over, it could mean a positive change in how the fund will perform in the future. If you don't know what to pick, then it may be time to get help from an outside advisor.

3. Self-directed brokerage account.
You will mostly find these at larger companies, but your employer may allow you to take all or some of your 401(k) and simply manage it yourself through the financial institution that handles your 401(k) plan. This option can be great for a savvy investor, or for someone

who truly wants to get hired help to really actively manage their 401(k). In this type of plan, you may be able to buy any type of mutual fund, exchange traded fund, stock, or bond giving you maximum choice and flexibility in your 401(k) plan.

When it comes to IRA (and Roth IRA) investing, there is truly a smorgasbord of different kinds of investment strategies. Remember that just because you opened your IRA at a bank, brokerage house, or insurance company, you are not required to leave that IRA where you originally opened the account. With IRA transfers, you can move that IRA to a new institution if you want to change advisors or investment strategy. Here are a few different ideas to think about for investing your IRA.

1. Do a core-satellite strategy.
Remember that IRAs can buy stocks, bonds, CDs, money markets, mutual funds, exchange-traded funds, and much more. Whether you buy mutual funds or exchange-traded funds (I am a bigger fan of indexing), the core part of your portfolio should represent a mixture of equity and bond-type funds that make an appropriate asset allocation for your risk tolerance and time frame to retirement. The important part here is to get the mix right and closely look at the expenses of what you are buying as cost eats into return. You can subscribe to a website like www.personalfund.com to see what your mutual funds are charging and get lower cost options. The core part of the portfolio should represent about 80% of the money. The satellite part of your portfolio will be where you take some risk and buy stock in individual companies or other investments where you can gain more upside potential. The satellite portion of the portfolio will represent about 20% of the money.

2. Real estate IRA.

I will say up front that you need to consult a really good CPA and closely read the IRS' rules related to prohibited transactions for IRA accounts. With commercial, residential, and land prices seeing significant drop in valuations, you may be able to pick up "real" real estate within your IRA account. You won't be able to have any personal use whatsoever with the real estate, but it isn't an option that most consider.

3. Private equity.

I am not a huge fan of private equity investing because it does not afford a lot of control and there are major liquidity issues. However, if you are going to take a risk for a portion of your retirement to go for the "home run," see if the private equity venture will allow you to use your IRA money. Due to the tough times of raising capital, more of the private equity ventures I have seen allow using IRA money. This may give you the opportunity to take a risk without having to liquidate current bank accounts. You should also review all of these options very carefully with a financial advisor, CPA, or attorney before making any decisions.

Since your IRA and 401(k) accounts will be the bulk of your retirement income in the future, take a step back in the first quarter of each year to see if you have the right strategy in place based on your risk tolerance, time frame, and other factors. It is important that you empower yourself by understanding what you are doing with your money – even if someone is giving you guidance along the way.

Take The Lump Sum Or The Pension?

You have spent 20 or 30 years working for the same company and now it's time to retire. You've put money away in your 401(k) and some other savings, but your really large asset is the pension plan where money has been put away for you all of these years. Your human resources or benefits department sends you a large packet of information telling you what options you have with your pension. Unbeknownst to you, they tell you that you can either get one check in a lump sum or they offer you various options if you choose a lifetime pension. So, what is the best direction to take with your pension plan?

Option 1:

Taking the pension. The first option you have is to take the pension. One of the things to consider is that taking the pension allows you to remove the stress of ever having to manage the money. Essentially, you are turning over your lump sum to an insurance company or the master pension fund and in return they are giving you a payout at a predetermined interest rate. When you make the decision to take the pension, it is normally a final decision. This means you can't go back a year later and ask for the lump sum because you changed your mind.

Generally, you will have several different payout options. The first is going to be a straight life pension. This will normally be your highest payout from the pension as it will pay you a monthly amount for the rest of your life. However, if you die three months later, the pension is gone permanently for your spouse or partner. A second option is to take a reduced pension with what is called an installment refund annuity or an annuity with period certain. Even though your payout amount will be lower with this option, it will guarantee the pension continues for a spouse or partner for a certain amount of years (5, 10, 20, etc.) or pay installments until the "lump sum" amount is met. The final option is a Joint with Rights of Survivorship election. This reduces your monthly pension payment by a significant amount, but it allows your spouse or partner to get either 50% or 75% of your pension in most cases for the rest of their lives should you predecease them.

While taking the pension can allow you remove the stress of managing the money and can offer a fixed monthly amount that you can't outlive, it is not without its drawbacks. The pension you receive may be guaranteed based upon the future financial stability of your employer. You will want to know what the reserves are in the pension fund and that it is backed by the Pension Benefit Guarantee Corporation (PBGC). Additionally, most pension payouts are not adjusted for inflation. If you begin taking payments at age 65, they may only be worth about half as much in 20 years if inflation moves along at 3% or more per year.

If you are really healthy at the time you take your pension, you may want to consider a pension maximization strategy which means taking the single life only pension choice, and then spending enough cash to buy a life insurance policy on yourself to recreate the survivor pension for your spouse if you die early. By using this strategy, if your spouse predeceases you, then you'll still have the full pension amount and possibly some additional cash value in an insurance policy.

Option 2:

Taking a lump sum. The second option you'll have is to take a lump sum. If you like the idea of controlling all of your assets versus the pension company having the assets, this can be an excellent option. When considering the lump sum option, you want to ensure you do a direct rollover into an IRA just like you would have with your 401(k) plan. If you took the pension as a lump sum of cash, you would be subject to adverse taxation (and possibly penalties depending on your age). Make sure you fill out the paperwork correctly, as this decision will be final once you elect it on your pension forms.

When you take the lump sum, one of the big advantages is that you now have access to your money. If you needed a larger chunk of cash for some reason throughout your retirement, the money is accessible to you at anytime. Your pension will now have a named beneficiary once your roll it over to an IRA, which means it will be there for a spouse, partner, or kids should you die. In addition, if you manage your account well, it could actually grow throughout your retirement while you distribute income from it at the same time.

However, taking the lump sum may not be all it's cracked up to be. The first thing you need to ensure is that you can find an investment strategy that will generate the necessary income throughout your retirement. The investments you choose may not be guaranteed like your pension. Additionally, if you put money in the stock market or other investments, you could run the risk of losing your principal which would be very costly once you retire since you won't have as many years to make up the losses. The last part of this equation is that the money is accessible to you. Sometimes, when money is in our pocket it can burn a hole in it from our excitement to go make new purchases. You need to really think about this lump sum as money to recreate your pension rather than buying items you need or want throughout retirement.

The decision. I highly recommended you get a qualified pension, tax, or financial advisor to help you run a thorough analysis before you make this your pension election. Remember, once you decide which route you will take, the decision is irreversible. Ultimately, you should be able to figure out what the real internal rate of return is on the pension if you choose the payout and then try to decide if you think you can build an investment portfolio that will do better than that rate.

Why Is It So Hard To Spend Money In Retirement?

The #1 concern for most people approaching retirement age is whether or not they will run out of money. It is such a great fear among individuals and families that many people actually deprive themselves of the objective they had for retirement: to have fun.

When you are working 40, 50, or 60 hours a week and raising a family, you often dream about what you will do when work is optional. You daydream about taking the vacations to destinations you have never seen. You ponder the idea of spending three months sitting beachside and purchasing that cool convertible you always wanted. So, what's stopping you? It isn't the kids. It isn't the work. It isn't the weather. Why is it so hard for retirees to enjoy the money they save for the very purpose of enjoying themselves when work becomes optional?

Without proper planning (and even sometimes with proper planning), the fact is that most retirees simply become paralyzed by the fear of running of out of money. Think about it: when you have been saving money and watching it grow for 30 or 40 years, the notion of spending money is a new skill that you'll need to learn. And training the spending muscle isn't easy.

It's really hard emotionally to see the account values of your brokerage accounts, IRA's, or 401(k) go down which is why most retirees ask the question about how much interest they can earn from their accounts. The moment a retiree sees their account values go down, they will begin to shrink their spending which is the main reason having a financial plan is paramount to making a successful and happy transition financially into retirement.

Consider these few final tips. After six months of spending money in retirement, did your checking/savings account go up or down? This is a good barometer of what's actually happening with your money. Have you considered what you are planning to leave to your kids down the road? If the answer is whatever is left over, then you should really start spending today. It will be harder than you think to spend all of your money especially if you have a pension. Lastly, don't deprive yourself. If you haven't been able to enjoy a few of the finer things in life, now is your time to start spending some money in retirement.

Getting Income from the Water Faucet

If you do a good job saving during your working career, the most difficult phase of retirement planning is the distribution phase. Since most people who think they are ready to financially retire worry about running out of money, figuring out the right way to take income from your investments is crucial. I think about retirement asset distribution much like a water faucet. You need to know which spigot to turn on in order to minimize taxation while you take home the most net income possible.

Remember that the first couple of years of retirement will generally result in a slightly larger amount of income needed before you settle into your regular expense mode. I have found that clients will spend more in the beginning of retirement, filling up the 2,000 hours of newly freed up time.

The age at which you begin the distribution phase will also have a large impact on which faucet you turn on to get your retirement income. Here are the three key areas and considerations for getting your income from the different faucets.

1. Fixed income

Fixed income can be received from different sources. The first may come from an employer pension. Pension plans need to be studied closely because the amount you receive from your employer may vary greatly if you take the benefit at the age of 55 versus the age of 65. In addition you need to make sure you understand if your pension has a cost of living adjustment. If your pension does not have a cost of living adjustment, then in essence you have a decreasing benefit each year. You will also need to consider whether you take a "life only" or a "joint with rights of survivor benefit" with the pension plan if you are married. This may affect immediate income to be slightly higher or lower based upon your decision. Serious analysis of the pension decision should be done before making a final choice on which route to go with the pension plan.

Social Security will be the other portion of your potential fixed income. For most people, the decision on what age to take social security is a complex one. One of the very critical items to review is whether or not you will be earning income from work if you decide to take social security early. Since there is a social security offset program in place, those still earning considerable waged income when they turn on this income stream can actually be detrimental to overall net income from this source. In today's environment, it is probably a good idea to plan for the cost of living adjustments on this income source to be less than the normal inflation rate.

2. Qualified retirement money.

This part of the faucet consists of your IRAs, 401(k)s, and generally other money you have been growing tax deferred for a long period of time. Most people are under the impression that you can only start accessing this money at the age of 59½, but by following the right procedures you could actually access this money earlier without an

IRS penalty of 10% (consult a good financial advisor or CPA before doing this). Since most of these assets have never been taxed before, you need to really plan on what your "net" number will be based upon current income tax brackets and your overall taxable income. One of the tougher retirement planning challenges for retirees is how to manage the overall investment strategy within their quali-fied plans. It is important for these assets to continue to generate income, but because assets will be taxable income (outside of Roth IRA's), a retiree needs to be thoughtful about what real net income they will actually come out of their qualified plans if they have other assets generating taxable income.

3. Required Minimum Distribution.
Keep a reminder that at the magical age of 70½, you will begin to have to take a forced distribution called a required minimum distribution.

4. Non-qualified assets.
The final faucet is made up of other assets such as bank accounts, CDs, brokerage accounts, real estate, and other liquid assets. I like the idea of having a year or two in cash when you are ready to make work optional since it allows you to not have an immediate worry about what investments you would have to use to generate income or which investments to liquidate. With non-qualified assets, you should consider what assets may trigger capital gains should you have to begin selling assets. Generally, selling your lowest performing, least taxed assets will likely be the best strategy if you have to liquidate these assets. Depending on the size of your estate, using different types of trusts may help you escape some of this taxation. Compar-ing how much net income (net of tax) from these assets versus using non-qualified assets is an important analysis for your financial advi-sor to do at the point you begin to generate retirement income.

Distribution is the most complex stage of retirement planning and should not be taken lightly. Since fixed income, qualified assets, and non-qualified assets work in concert during the distribution phase, you should do plenty of analysis so you can maximize the use of your assets. This planning will help relieve some of the fear of running out of money, and will ultimately allow you to figure out the income level you can truly sustain during retirement.